# THE KNOTTY

## A Musical Documentary

Introduction
and Notes by

PETER CHEESEMAN

First published in 1970
by Methuen & Co Ltd
11 New Fetter Lane London EC4
Introduction and notes copyright ©
Peter Cheeseman 1970
Text of The Knotty copyright ©
The Victoria Theatre Company 1970

Printed by Redwood Press Ltd
Trowbridge, Wiltshire

SBN 416 07970 9

A long-playing record of THE
KNOTTY (ARGO RECORD ZTR125)
has been issued by the Argo Record
Company.

## Methuen Playscripts

The Methuen Playscripts series exists
to extend the range of plays in print by
publishing work which is not yet widely
known but which has already earned a
place in the acting repertoire of the
modern theatre.

## The Knotty

The Knotty is a 'musical documentary', first
presented at the Victoria Theatre, Stoke-on-
Trent in 1966 and revived there in 1967 and
1969, when it was also presented at the
Florence Rassegna Internazionale dei Teatri
Stabili.

'The Knotty' is the local affectionate name
for the North Staffordshire Railway, begun in
1845 and amalgamated in 1923 with the London
Midland and Scottish Railway (its badge was
the Staffordshire Knot). The play tells its
history and was created by the Victoria Theatre
Company, working from historical research
by Peter Terson under the direction of Peter
Cheeseman.

The Knotty has proved to be one of the most
successful of the 'regional documentaries'
presented in theatres outside London during
the past five years. This edition contains a
full introduction by Peter Cheeseman, describing the working methods of the Victoria
Company and notes indicating some of the
sources of the material included in the play,
which ranged from Victorian newspaper
cuttings to the reminiscences of many of the
men who worked on 'Old Knotty'.

OTHER METHUEN PLAYSCRIPTS

THE KNOTTY, a musical documentary about the life and death of
the North Staffordshire Railway, was created in 1966 after research
by Peter Terson and Peter Cheeseman, by the following company of
actors and actresses, directed by Peter Cheeseman

> Gillian Brown
> Edward Clayton
> Ellis Dale
> Ron Daniels
> Anjula Harman
> Harry Jones
> Peter King
> Christopher Martin
> Susan Pitts
> Anne Raitt

> and guest artist, folk singer Jeff Parton

The show was first presented on 12 July 1966

The production was revived in 1967 and 1969, with some changes of
cast due to changes in the permanent company. Gillian Brown,
Christopher Martin, Anne Raitt and Jeff Parton were in the cast
throughout. Other artists who have appeared in the show are (1967)
Terence Davies, David Hill, Robert French, Susan Glanville,
James Hayes and Jane Wood – Robert French created the new Oak
Farm scene as printed here – and (1969) Christopher Bond, Geoffrey
Larder, Susan Tracy, Arthur Whybrown and Brian Young.

A total of 84 performances of THE KNOTTY were given at the
Victoria Theatre, one in Cardiff at the invitation of the Welsh Arts
Council. In May 1969 five performances were given in Florence,
Italy as the British contribution to their international festival of
permanent theatre companies (Rassegna Internazionale dei Teatri
Stabili)

INTRODUCTION

## DOCUMENTARY THEATRE AT STOKE–ON–TRENT

### A Performance not a Play

Children at school are no longer exclusively directed to regard
theatre as animated literature. Though there are university
professors still living who would have Shakespeare intoned in a
flat monotone to permit the uninterrupted appreciation of all the
resonances of meaning echoing round every immortal line, it is
almost commonplace to hear the most academic of teachers assert
that plays can only be understood in performance. The currency
of this very liberal opinion has made it possible to consider producing this volume, for the text of THE KNOTTY presented in the
following pages is an attempt to describe a typical one of nearly
a hundred performances of the show. The result could not really
be called literature, nor have I imagined that anyone else would
ever want to perform THE KNOTTY. What we do know is that the
growing interest in theatre documentary seems to justify publishing
a detailed description of one which worked quite well, both as a
Do–It–Yourself guide for professionals and amateurs who want to
take advantage of our experiences, and as a useful record for
students of the theatre. As the latter are now happily as numerous
as students of woodwork, and not even the worst educated person
can avoid being a student of theatre before he escapes from school,
we hope it will be an interesting book for quite a lot of people.

### Documentaries and Plays

This introduction, is not an attempt to define what I think the word
DOCUMENTARY means nor what I think DOCUMENTARY THEATRE
should be. It is an attempt to describe and define some shows we
have done in Stoke–on–Trent which seemed to suit the description
DOCUMENTARY rather than PLAY. THE KNOTTY is one of these.

Both in theory and in practice we have found that the value of our
experiences in putting on these shows lay in discovering and
following certain creative disciplines which clearly distinguished
them from plays. The difference is sometimes one of degree rather
than kind but is none the less a difference which all of us find
makes a stimulating contribution to the life of the theatre, for
actors, audiences, directors and the playwrights who write plays
for us.

I use the word CONTRIBUTION advisedly because many writers
construe the present fashion for documentary theatre as an attack

on the status and validity of the writer in the theatre. May I emphatically disassociate myself from such a viewpoint and admit I cannot share the intolerance of writers' plays which some of my professional theatre colleagues have expressed in order to propose the excellence of documentaries. In any one year here we present about fourteen new productions, of which only one is likely to be a documentary like THE KNOTTY. The rest are plays, about half of them by living writers working closely with us, often on the theatre staff. If it were possible, in terms of human effort, to make one more of the fourteen a documentary I might propose it, but no more than that. It is impossible to say shortly why I feel that the PLAY remains for me the major and mainstream theatrical form but it is an important issue. I will try to make clear my attitude to the documentaries gradually in what follows. If I add that in many cases what I advance as a reason for our doing these shows is also a good reason for not doing more than one a year of them, then perhaps that will answer.

The growth of documentary theatre seems an inevitable part of our twentieth-century scientific enthusiasm for a particular relationship with facts, and a kind of intolerance and suspicion of the products of the imagination. It is too widespread to be construed as another aspect of British Puritanism, though I am certain that that baleful influence intensifies it at certain points. Photographic and electronic camera and tape recorder have helped to bring about documentary theatre, both by suggesting appropriate genres in the media they have created, and by their direct use in the theatre itself. Projected pictures, still and moving, can provide an important element in most documentary theatre, along with the tape-recorded voice. Here at Stoke, the tape recorder is a key element in collecting source material during the research period but also directly provides some of the elements of performance, speech and sound effects. The tape recorder gave us on-stage horses and cannon in THE STAFFORDSHIRE REBELS, electric trams in SIX INTO ONE, trains in THE KNOTTY and a volcano in THE BURNING MOUNTAIN. (Actually our Stromboli was the sound of Apollo XII blasting off: as in the show Stromboli was Hugh Bourne's vision of Hell the decision seemed justified. Such qualms do weigh heavily on us in the documentaries, as the patient reader will discover.) Documentary theatre seems inevitable in an age dominated by scientific investigation and technological invention. But it also seems part of our passion for getting down to the truth, seeing behind the scenes. Is it also part of our response to the evasion and humbug of Victorian social morality, one of our answers to our grandfathers who draped piano legs for decency's sake?

Whatever the motives, everybody seems to want to do it, and inevitably in tht theatre there is a lot of loose talk about it, a lot of attitudinising and a lot of imprecision. The theatre is a terrible place for pretending to do things when you're not. That's what it's all about I suppose, but it shouldn't spread off the stage into our trade descriptions. It is becoming a fashionable theatrical virtue to be doing a documentary (which is why the authors are getting so cross) but really a great deal of what are being called 'documentaries' are only historical or contemporary plays in which the names of the characters on the stage are the same as the ones they had in real life. Calling such plays documentaries doesn't make them any better than they are and is both confusing and a little tiresome. Every writer I have worked with sets down personal experience and puts himself and his acquaintances recognisably into his plays, changing their names, setting one man and his speeches down verbatim and recognisably, cutting into bits to make a bit of one man a bit of another woman and part of yet another incident. Yet I wouldn't call any of their plays DOCUMENTARIES. Shakespeare used bits of historical source material (as well as other literature) liberally. In JULIUS CAESAR he drew frequently from Sir Thomas North's translation of the Greek historian Plutarch. Here is Plutarch on the historical Marcus Brutus (the comparison is by T.S.Dorsch):

> 'I dare assure thee, that no enemy hath taken nor shall take Marcus Brutus alive, and I beseech God keep him from that fortune: for wheresoever he be found, alive or dead, he will be found like himself.'

Here is now Shakespeare's Brutus speaking (Viv 21-5)

> 'I dare assure thee that no enemy
> Shall ever take alive the noble Brutus.
> The gods defend him from so great a shame!
> When you do find him, or alive or dead,
> He will be found like Brutus, like himself.'

But I don't think anybody could claim that JULIUS CAESAR was an unmusical documentary, even though a lot of it was nicked from a history book. I make this point because I believe the distinction between play and documentary to be an important one, and worth exploring in practice. I don't believe there is anything to be gained from being confused about it all.

## Particular origins of the Stoke Documentaries

THE KNOTTY and all our documentary work at Stoke-on-Trent have quite particular and deliberately local motives and quite particular characteristics. The principal motive derives from the basic policy of the Victoria Theatre. This was opened in October

1962 as the permanent home of the Studio Theatre Company founded
in 1955 by Stephen Joseph to do new plays and explore the possibilities of theatre in the round. Stephen's policy inevitably and
deliberately led to the presence of writers in the company, which
lived by touring theatreless towns from 1955 to 1962. The company
was very small indeed – on the average three actors, two actresses, two stage managers and a manager. It was not uncommon
to find two of this number were dramatists, contributing plays to
the company's repertoire. Writers including Robert Bolt and James
Saunders provided plays from outside the company, but inside it
for most of its touring life from the early years were Alan Ayckbourn and David Campton, both of whom for a time earned their
keep three times over, working as actors and writers as well as
stage manager and manager respectively. When the Victoria
Theatre opened in 1962 under my direction David Campton had left
the company to earn his living as a full-time writer but Alan
Ayckbourn became a member of the new permanent company of four
men and two women. (Two of the other actors incidentally were
David Halliwell and novelist Peter King, though neither had started
to write plays at that stage.)

The presence of a writer working in the company seemed to me to
provide an essential factor in the creative potency of the group.
I have worked with teams of actors who never meet writers at all,
who get their scripts by post. If they ever happen to do a new play
their attitude to the text is curiously immature. They begin by
treating every phrase, each comma, with a kind of superstitious
reverence. As they begin really to come to grips with the text and
discover its difficulties the magic evaporates overnight and is
replaced by casual contempt 'Bloody unspeakable dialogue' they
say at a coffee break explosion. 'Cut the whole bloody scene if
you ask me...' and so on. If the writer actually appears he gets
the same treatment, going from god to goblin in a fortnight (mark
you, with icy courtesy towards the end.) A company which has a
writer working in it tends to behave differently. As with their
actor colleagues, working together over long periods tends to
create a simple and healthy respect for each others' abilities, a
sensible awareness of shortcomings. All are aware of the ARBIT-
RARINESS of many creative decisions and are therefore in the
right position to see and respect skill and craftsmanship. The
writer in this situation is treated as an equal by a company who
will tend to co-operate fully in the process of realising his play,
and commit themselves entirely to it. They become true partners
in the creative enterprise, the play develops much more in rehearsal, performance has a strength and impact difficult to achieve
where a company cannot participate in this way.

The documentaries at Stoke began as a direct result of Alan Ayckbourn's leaving the company in the Spring of 1964 to work on an ill-fated London production of his play MR WHAT-NOT which he had created with the Victoria Company. Peter Terson had only just begun to write for us but didn't live yet in Stoke-on-Trent. For the first time in nearly ten years there was no writer on the staff. I sat one morning in a run-through of Shaw's CANDIDA which I was directing, and my mind wandered around the problem.

We were getting on for eighteen months old at Stoke and there were a number of things I hadn't begun to tackle that needed beginning. Though we were dedicated to the idea of giving expression to the life of our new home community we had found no local writer and had no means of using local subject matter. I thought of us as a 'group theatre' but had not yet found any artistic format in which we could really give creative reality to this ideal. In the theatre I consider that if you believe in anything it must be given expression on your stage: otherwise it doesn't exist. I wanted us also to begin to bridge the cultural gap which separates the artist from the majority of the community and which I believe to be a gap created by style not subject matter. I wanted to begin to develop a popular language, a style of our own which would make theatre livelier and more attractive than the current conventional play format.

Years of working in the exciting creative freedom of theatre in the round under Stephen Joseph's intelligent and imaginative leadership had already enabled David Campton and Alan Ayckbourn to develop racy theatrical narratives which had just reached a comic peak in Alan's brilliant MR WHATNOT. This play was, moreover, a true and uncompromising piece of self-expression by a group of young artists. No excuses, no indulgence were needed to appreciate it. Cursed with the currency of psychological realism, most of us in regional theatre, working with few older actors and actresses, have had to prod on youngsters drenched in white powder and with painted faces, pretending to a maturity that disappears in the cloud of white dust which every violent encounter provokes. MR WHATNOT vindicated an approach which took a fair and square look at all our limitations. Alan threw naturalistic casting to the winds, exploited the vigorous and dedicated youthfulness of the company, its flexible professional training, and created a real work of art out of our manifest poverty. At Stoke it was our first great popular success, and though it lured Alan Ayckbourn away from us, it demanded we meet its challenge without him and pick up where he had left off.

Alan so far has shown himself at his best as an ingenious and whimsical comedian. I tend to be a bit serious and guiltily academic, I think subconsciously making up for all the essays I still owe the history master and all the lectures I missed at Sheffield. ('Where is Mr Cheeseman?' my tutor John Danby once said while I was directing KING LEAR 'Is he dead?') It seems inevitable that the solution that strangely clicked into my mind in the dusty old church hall we were rehearsing in (there was an immovable set on our acting area that week) should have been one that derived from the didactic Left Wing theatre brilliantly extended by Joan Littlewood out of the German and American documentary traditions. If we had no writer amongst us, we must assume the function collectively, as a group, shape our own material out of documentary research into the history of this community. The process should be one in which we, the actual practitioners, dominated the presentation of the material. The aim should be to use all our performing experience to create a lively and popular show and a loose format for future development. We should put the show on at the end of the season before our fortnight of annual holiday, in the middle of empty-seated July, to give the summer some kind of climax to build up to.

## The Jolly Potters

When we broke for lunch we took the opportunity of proximity to a cosy local Bass house to drop in for a drink. The landlord Doug Birks is a great joker. He struck a dramatic attitude as we made for the bar, 'And the title of your next play is' he declared 'THE JOLLY POTTERS'. It was the name of his pub and of a number of other locals. It was the obvious title for our first local documentary. All that remained was to create one which fitted that title. Ultimately we did, finding it a useful irony for a show which centred round the miserable working conditions of the nineteenth-century potworkers and the 1842 Chartist riots.

## Four more Documentaries

We have produced more or less one documentary a year since 1964. THE STAFFORDSHIRE REBELS (1965) was about the Civil War in the county. Bradshaw and Harrison were local men. Charles II's celebrated escaping adventures after the battle of Worcester mainly took place in South Staffs. THE KNOTTY was our third, in 1966. In 1967, Arnold Bennett's

centenary year, we completed the research for a bio-
graphical documentary on Bennett only to get thrown out of
the theatre in the administrative row which ultimately and
tragically separated us from Stephen Joseph at the beginning of his fatal illness. We kept THE KNOTTY going
until 1968 when we made SIX INTO ONE about the battles
over a kind of Maud proposal of the 1900's – Federation of
the Six pottery towns. In January 1970 we made THE
BURNING MOUNTAIN – the story of the Hugh Bourne, the
North Staffordshire wheelwright, and his great revival
movement, the Primitive Methodists. Throughout, the
original motives have remained, plus an obvious decision
to explore the potential of the ACTOR as the principal
instrument of the documentary rather than relying on a kind
of tension between the actor and projected photographs to
provided the documentary veracity. In our simply converted
theatre in the round projection is technically complex and
expensive. It seemed to me in any case not to be an essential
element of theatre documentary, though the development of
a new and special style of acting which honestly exposed the
factual quality of the material did. This we have worked on,
and I try to describe a little of it below.

## Music

An obvious problem for me in following in the footsteps of
Joan Littlewood was the fact that the success of OH WHAT A
LOVELY WAR depended on the presence of a number of
talented and inventive variety artists in the cast, capable of
enlivening all kinds of material by their own invention and
trade skill. (Victor Spinetti's hilarious, grim and bawdy
bayonet training sketch is a good example). I had to exploit
the companies' own capacities and special skills as actors.
The job that has taken longest to do in this respect is coping
with the, for me, necessary musical element in the show.
The first theatre documentary I saw, a Living Newspaper
about Joe Hill the American trade union leader, left me with
a firm belief that music was essential to provide an emotional
momentum in a theatrical situation packed with heterogeneous
factual material and very short of characters that run through
more than one or two scenes in two dozen. THE JOLLY
POTTERS was made possible with the help of THE KEELE
ROW, a small folk group mostly from our nearby university,
whose members also played in THE STAFFORDSHIRE REBELS
But one of the best singers in that show was an actor in the
company, Ben Kingsley, and in 1966 I began to look de-

liberately and with some optimism for good artists who could also sing. For THE KNOTTY the only musician was Jeff Parton, a local folk singer, and instrumentalist, the show leaning heavily on the superb singing of two actresses in the company, Gillian Brown and Anne Raitt. In SIX INTO ONE we were joined by Guillaume Oyono Mbia, a young African dramatist who played the talking drum and the accordion. In THE BURNING MOUNTAIN the cast was trained in un-accompanied part song by a talented young local musician, Stuart Johnson. Apart from recorder intros, they managed on their own. But we're still waiting for a good actor who is also a superb instrumentalist for the next show.

## The Creative Process

It is now necessary to say something about the techniques we have evolved for creating these documentaries, since it is these creative techniques that distinguish them from the plays in our repertoire.

## Preliminary Research

The process is like a kind of inverted pyramid, gradually involving more and more people till the middle of rehearsals, when the entire company is directly contributing to the making of the show. It begins with the research period, lasting about six months, during which the chosen subject is investigated, first of all in books about it, then in all the primary source material we can uncover – original documents, diaries, letters newspaper articles, together with tape-recorded interviews with participants in the events. (For THE KNOTTY we inter-viewed former railwaymen who'd worked on the North Staf-fordshire Railway, for SIX INTO ONE we interviewed retired civic officers and councillors who had been involved, as well as a selection of inhabitants of the Federated Six Towns, town by town. For THE BURNING MOUNTAIN we interviewed many Christians and non-Christians as well as Primitive Methodists about their beliefs and superstitions.) These recordings are summarised, and some are totally transcribed. The other research material is noted, catalogued, and photo-graphed where necessary.

## Research Committee

This work has been first of all done by myself as director of all these shows, and by the resident dramatist, who operates under the strict discipline of not being permitted to write any of the show himself. As we get to within three months of production, planning of plays in the repertoire is organised to provide a very small cast play immediately before the documentary. The remainder of the company of seven actors and four actresses, who will not be involved in the daily rehersals of this small cast play, form a kind of committee of the company who are as soon as possible involved in the research. (It is necessary to explain here for the non-professional reader that in all regional theatre companies the number of artists is only large enough to allow plays to be put on by casting all of them, or most of them in each play. Rehersals begin at 10 am and continue except for a lunch break till about 5 pm. After the break for tea the company must then prepare for the evening show. In our case this happens for fifty out of the fifty-two weeks in a year. Time tends to be our most precious creative necessity: it is always short.)

The resident dramatist and I meet and talk to the research committee, who then read all the research summaries and abstracts to date, and listen to any tapes made so far. They then take on responsibility for certain research topics and we all work together in regular discussions to try and evolve a shape for the story. So far as possible we try not to discuss it in theatrical terms till we are sure of the shape the subject matter itself seems to fall into.

## Primary Source Material – The Self-imposed Rule

One important discipline now emerges. The material used on the stage must be primary source material. Words or actions deriving from the events to be described or participants in those events are the only permitted material for the scenes of the documentary. If there is no primary source material available on a particular topic, no scene can be made about it.

The whole distinct character of these shows derives from this self-imposed rule and the way in which every piece of material, every idea for a scene, is tested against it. It is a rule that ensures that a multiplicity of voices are heard in the documentary, as opposed to the play, in which all the characters really speak with the voice of the dramatist and, as Professor G Wilson Knight puts it in his distinguished book, THE WHEEL OF FIRE, the persons ultimately are not human at all, but purely symbols of a poetic vision'

The fact that the process of creation of the text of the documentary is controlled by a group of people, even under fairly strong leadership, rather than just by one person, also tends to preserve the contradiction of viewpoint inherent in every historical event, controlled as it is by a number of people. Critics of the practice of doing the documentary this way tend to scoff at the idea of plays by committees, and dislike the result, as do the tidy-minded. The reader (though preferably the spectator) must judge for himself.

## Text Created in Rehearsals

At the end of the research period, rehearsals begin. In the early years we only ended up with three weeks but we've managed to win four and even five in recent years as expanding audiences have enabled some shows to run longer. By this time we on the research committee have a proposed story and a kind of theatrical shape in which to tell it. This will consist of a running list, detailing the subject of each scene and song and the order in which they will appear in the show. To each item on the list will be attached particular pieces of primary source material from which this scene must be made. As we work through the show, members of the research committee take charge of particular scenes and songs and often rehearse these themselves, producing them for inspection in a rough shape on the stage. How this happened in THE KNOTTY, with both scenes and songs, I try to illustrate in the notes following the text. The first rehearsal of each scene consists of a massive carve-up of its source material. This can often be a physically difficult session to cope with as it may involve handing round several large photographs of newspaper pages to various characters scattered round the stage, or large sheets stuck with pieces cut out of a number of transcribed sources by the members of the research committee. A special production secretary sits at these initial rehearsals. As soon as some kind of line develops, and speeches are apportioned, and the main moves or business of the scene settled in this session, she makes a first script of the scene. Then rehearsing it is just like rehearsing any new plays except that there tends to be a great deal more cutting and modification of it before the end – always bearing in mind that such editing must keep pieces of source material intact. In fact this is the crux of the problem. Primary source material can be cut and edited into very small chunks, pieces from heterogeneous sources can be juxtaposed in a scene (providing we make it clear in the show that this is what we are doing) and however complex the process, each piece of the material retains its original flavour and quality, and can exude this on stage. But the moment passages are totally dismantled, down to their

constituent words, and re-assembled, then the process becomes writing, and is no longer valid for us in a documentary.
As can be seen in the notes, the most that happens in this
region is the addition of the odd word, linking phrase, or
greeting, to join passages together. Sometimes the tense of
a verb has to be altered. But the great bulk of the source
material remains edited but not dismantled. During the
creative phase we are all asking one another the questions
'Can we do this?' 'Is this permissible?' It is a curious fact
that even new members of the company know the answer
almost before they have finished phrasing the question, and
know the moment when what they do ceases to become an imaginative penetration of the source material and starts to tell
a plain lie about a man or an event.

## Songs

The composition of the songs that play an important part in
these shows is not quite subject to the same disciplines.
Usually the songs have a narrative function and do not actually
depict an event. In this case they stand outside the action and
can if necessary, I feel, contain our own comments embodied
in our own writing, though it is important that there are rarely
more than two written and composed by the same people.
Where possible we try to use songs of the period we are
dealing with, usually folk songs. I find folk songs accessible
and attractive to more sections of the public than any other
kind of music. They also do not reduce words to a subservient
relationship with the music, so never become a gap in the action
by a lapse into mere decoration. Also where we have to use a
piece of narrative to fill a gap in the action we now tend to
use song rather than the extensive recorded announcements
which THE KNOTTY and the previous documentaries employed. Any new songs composed for the documentaries are
either set to folk tunes or composed in the musical language
of that tough tradition.

## A Controlled Emergency

The absence of any complete script at the beginning of rehearsals, and the sheer necessity of providing a cracking show
at the end remains a frightening situation though each year
we seem to get away with it. It is in one sense a deliberately
contrived and controlled emergency which every year I try
to make more efficient without losing its essential and
stimulating thrill. The lengthy and thorough research period

is vital. The material is there. We are used to working to a deadline. The total challenge of imaginatively recreating factual material in an exciting way usually tends to bring the best out of everyone in the company.

The greatest enemy is inefficiency, but I find this is something that can be prepared for and avoided. The subtlest enemy is failure of courage: I know I have made my worst mistakes through artistic cowardice more than anything else. I remember in directing an adaptation of Bennett's CLAY-HANGER a situation very similar to the kind that crops up in a documentary. We decided to include the crucial scene where Edwin saves his father's first-floor printing room when a new machine threatens to cave the floor in. Edwin dashes onto the dangerous floor and ties off a rope to hold everything up. There were twenty-five fast-moving scenes and no printing press possible. Though I knew in my heart that I should rely completely on the movement of Edwin, his father and the printing shop workers edging up against the walls to convey the existence of machinery and danger, I larded up the scene with fancy lighting and sound effects which were quite superfluous and much less effective. But in fact the documentaries present so many problems like this that cowardice becomes almost out of the question without abandoning the show, though the fear tempts one to tidy solutions nearly as often as it stimulates an imaginative answer. But we usually manage to avoid the temptation. The first show in 1964 was a truly frightening experience, but it never seems to become anything less than more difficult, though less frightening each time. Ultimately the show is a total test of the entire company: every member finds out before long that it depends on how much they are prepared to do on their own, without supervision, to make sure that every scene and song gets created in the first place and adequately rehearsed in the second. It is a practical point worth making here that many scenes have to be planned with small and different casts so that about four or more can be rehearsing simultaneously all over the theatre.

## Special Acting Style

A word needs to be said now about the style of performance we have developed for these shows. First of all, as the actor is the means of exposing factual material he must have a totally candid and honest basic relationship with the audience to start with. It is almost as if this permitted the audience to trace on him the shape of each character when they could see it so clearly standing out against his own openness. There needs then to be considerable restraint and objectivity in the playing of each part. There is a point perceptible where extravagance of characterisation clearly begins to direct the attention of the audience away from the narrative line. Such extravagance must be avoided. This kind of restraint seems also to affect the conventions of the mime used in these shows, which needs to be almost laconic in its lack of elaboration. A good example of this was provided in the Pole Dance in THE KNOTTY, where the movement had to have the poker faced simplicity of Celtic dancing. It is a kind of mime with the hands in the pockets and the face straight. It matches also with the lack of operatic expressiveness demanded in the proper singing of folk songs, throwing so much weight on words and story in the song.

## Costume

Finally the actors are dressed in costumes which for the most part permit modification for different characters by superficial changes of hat, neckwear, or jacket. In THE KNOTTY the girls wore plain dresses in a heavy tweedy material, coarse enough to look homespun and hardwearing, but heavy enough to look grand depending on whether they crouched in a shawl or put on an elaborate headdress and mantle. The men wore black serge railway trousers, black boots, white shirts, and a multiplicity of hats, jackets and neckwear as they worked through the play. Changes were often done on stage, while going off from a scene, or sitting on the seven-inch step in front of the front row. These techniques again deliberately relate each character to the actor as common denominator and help to preserve the documentary approach.

## Performance

Usually after an agonising final weekend of doubt and uncertainty the show goes on, and is played in our district in a kind of atmosphere of participation that is almost impossible to describe. We have never made any compromise in the direction of making the shows comprehensible to people from outside the district. There is no point – they are our special contribution to its life, and any visitor who drops in must expect to feel like a visitor. I believe myself that an aim as

specific as this is likely to be much more creatively fruitful
than one which seeks to please the nation – or the world.
These are both almost incomprehensible abstractions of
which we can only have a    kind of mathematical or spatial
awareness. The only human situations we can truly compre-
hend are the ones small enough for us to feel a significant
or effective part of. Otherwise our actual sense of existing
at all is depressingly diminished.

Paradoxically enough, shows which were ruthlessly narrowed
in their address to our own home community turn out to be
the ones which other districts want to see, and our experience
of playing THE KNOTTY in other places, even as far as Italy,
on our rare tours from home, has been that the particularity
of the product does not seem to create any kind of difficulty
of comprehension, only a special flavour that strangers find
attractive. The Florentines appeared to get as much out of
THE KNOTTY as an audience at home.

## Response to the Documentaries

The documentaries have had two important influences. First of
all they have been the means through which North Staffordshire
people have realised we were serious about our attachment
to the district. Even that huge mass of people who don't come
to the theatre and never intend to seems to contain a large
number who regard us fiercely as a cherished local possession.
In our pioneering for the attention of the majority this is a
welcome start. The other potent influence of the shows has
been on our associated dramatists. It had always been my hope
in 1964 that when we did get dramatists into the company again,
these shows, first developed to fill their absence, would
provide valuable examples of styles and theatrical techniques,
derived from our own performing experience, that writers
might be persuaded to exploit themselves. This has happened,
particularly in the case of Peter Terson and Ken Campbell,
the two writers who have so far worked most closely with us.
Terson's ZIGGER-ZAGGER is the direct result of his experiences in working on THE KNOTTY, and none of his
subsequent work is free from an influence that has widened
his theatrical vocabulary. Ken Campbell has developed many
characteristics of these shows in his own way – in the whole
tone and style of JACK SHEPPARD (produced in London under
the title ANYTHING YOU SAY WILL BE TWISTED) and in
the highly original work he is now developing in his road
show – an informal touring entertainment in which a small

group of actors use the style of the Stoke documentaries to
mount a series of hilarious and sometimes disturbing dramat
anecdotes.

## Education

Finally it is obvious that the way in which the documentaries
are created at Stoke-on-Trent has an interesting educationa
application. The whole process is rather like a class projec
and it is clear that children could make exciting contact with
historical and contemporary documentary material in the job
of dramatising it. I would like to make two points about this.
First, no performance objective is necessary in order to ma
the project exciting – certainly not anyway a formal public p
formance. A small group can work quite happily within its
own boundaries in tackling this material. Otherwise exposur
to groups in the same class or stream is sufficient to add a
kind of performance excitement to the process. Second,
teachers with whom I discuss this topic modestly express
fears that clever professionals can perhaps cope with the
imaginative invention needed to realise this material in an
exciting way. Our own experience in working informally with
children on documentary material clearly indicates that if
they are really given the responsibility, they themselves
provide the imagination.

Peter Cheeseman


## Illustrations

The illustrations in the centre section show scenes from
The Knotty in rehearsal and performance. Plates 1,2,3,4,
5,6 and 8 are from photographs by Richard Smiles. The
photograph in Plate 7 and the photographs on the back of
the cover, showing Peter Cheeseman and Harry Sharratt in
rehearsal with some of the cast, and Peter Terson talking
to a railwayman at one of the loop line stations, are by Ian
Stone. All the photographs are reproduced by courtesy of
the Victoria Theatre Company, Stoke-on-Trent.

All illustrations are of the 1969 production except
No 7 which is of the first 1967 production.

# The Knotty

## The Setting

The Victoria Theatre is constructed as a theatre in the round. Steeply raked blocks of seating five and six rows deep surround an acting area seven inches below the level of the front row. The steep rake gives the floor of the acting area great prominence. For Part One of THE KNOTTY a light coloured stage cloth covers the floor, designed like a simplified old map showing no more than the long and indented triangular shape of the valley up which the railway is to run, and the initial letters of the names of the Six Potteries Towns stretche along it, together with an N for Newcastle-under-Lyme at one side. There are three main entrances for the actors, between the seating blocks. Two are in adjacent corners of the rectangle the seating makes, one in the centre of the opposite side. A low four foot square rostrum is placed on the edge of the acting area opposite this centre entrance. The folk singer sits here and it is used as a kind of orchestra pit throughout the show for other artists who sing or play on it. On the acting area four low wooden stools and four wooden chairs are scattered.

Instruments are tuned up by Anne Raitt and Jeff Parton sitting on the rostrum. The first sound of the show itself however comes from the large loudspeaker cluster hanging centrally over the acting area –

# Part One

SOUND OF A DIESEL ENGINE APPROACHING AND
DRAWING UP AT A PLATFORM. BRAKES, THROBBING
AS ENGINE TICKS OVER.

LOUDSPEAKER ANNOUNCEMENT: This is Stoke-on-
Trent. Station Announcer calling. The train now
standing at platform one is the fourteen-forty to
Stafford, calling at Barlaston and Stone, then Staf-
ford. There are connections at Stafford for London,
Euston.

HONK OF DIESEL HORN. SOUND OF TRAIN DRAW-
ING AWAY. HOUSE LIGHTS FADE. SPOTLIGHT ON
SINGER.


INTRODUCTION SONG

JEFF (UNACCOMPANIED): There's a story I will tell
you, if you'll listen to my song,
I hope that it will please you, and it will not keep
you long.
I'll tell you how the railway through the Potteries
was planned,
How the N.S.R. was built and changed the face of
the land.

I will tell you of George Stephenson, that engineer
so fine,
I'll tell you of the navvies that worked upon the line.
From Crewe to Stoke and Derby the rails they were
laid,
And through Hanley, Burslem, Tunstall, the Loop
Line it was made.

STAGE BRIGHTENS, REST OF CAST ENTER, IN
EARLY NINETEENTH-CENTURY COSTUME. FOUR
WOMEN, SIX MEN.

You will hear how the railwaymen for Unions cam-
paigned,
And of the Great World War that laid so many in
their graves,

And then Amalgamation with the L.M.S. at last
Made the great days of 'The Knotty' just an echo in
the past.

COACH DRIVER HONKS PERMANENT WAY MAN'S
HORN. MANDOLINE AND GUITAR ACCOMPANIMENT
BEGINS:

## COACH SCENE

ALL SING: He that will not merry, merry be
With a generous bowl and toast.
May he in Bridewell be shut up
And fast bound to a post.
Let him be merry, merry, merry there,
And we will be merry, merry here,
For who can know where we may go
To be merry another year.

COACH DRIVER (HONK): December the fifteenth, eighteen
hundred and ten. Advertisement. London, Liverpool,
Birmingham, Bristol. Coaches will set off from the
Shakespeare Inn, Newcastle every day at one o'clock
at noon...arriving at the Saddle Inn, Liverpool at nine
o'clock the same evening.

POSH GENTLEMAN LOOKS AT HIS WATCH.

POSH GENT: Bong.

COACH DRIVER: Honk.

INSTRUMENTAL BEGINS AGAIN. ACTORS MOVE
AROUND MAKING A COACH OUT OF THE CHAIRS
AND STOOLS. AS THEY DO SO THEY SING 'BONG'
TO THE TUNE AND SIT IN THE COACH. THEY MOVE
AND SING DECOROUSLY.

FIRST YOUNG MAN: Fares to Liverpool, inside coach
with the gentry, sixteen shillings.

SECOND YOUNG MAN: Fares to Liverpool, outside
coach, with the weather, nine shillings.

THEY CLIMB UP ONTO STOOLS BEHIND THE
SEATED PASSENGERS

COACH DRIVER: Honk.

ALL WAGGLE WITH THE JOLTING OF THE COACH

AS THEY SING.

ALL SING: He that will not merry, merry be
And take his glass in course,
May be be obliged to drink small beer,
Ne'er a penny in his purse.
Let him be merry, merry, merry there
And we will be merry merry here
For who can know where we may go
To be merry another year.

COACH DRIVER: Look out!

HE STANDS ON HIS STOOL.

LADIES STAND AND SCREAM.

POSH GENT: Good heavens!

CRASH SOUND. ALL FLUNG ONTO STAGE IN ALL
DIRECTIONS. CHAIRS OVERTURNED. DRIVER
CONTROLS HORSES.

COACH DRIVER: Woah!

NIGHT FALLS, INJURED PASSENGERS GROAN
AND SLOWLY GET UP.

FIRST YOUNG MAN (LIMPING): I was travelling by the
very fast and much improved coach from Newcastle
to Liverpool, when one of the wheels suddenly went to
pieces, and had it not been for the care and attention
of the coachman, many of the passengers must have
been seriously injured, and some would have lost their
lives without doubt. Here then is a proof of the typical
neglect of the coach contractors.

TWO HIGHWAYMEN ENTER WITH MASKS AND PISTOLS.

HIGHWAYMEN: Stand and deliver!

THEY SYSTEMATICALLY FRISK ALL, RECEIVING
GOODS AS DESCRIBED.

COACH DRIVER: We were yesterday evening stopped by
two armed men on foot, on our way from Newcastle, who
took from John Pass a red Morocco notebook, containing
sixty-five pounds and from another a silver watch with
the day of the month on the face, the hour and the
minute fingers were of steel, the maker's name in the
inside, Bannister of Lichfield.

POSH GENT: The man who robbed John Pass appeared to be about five feet ten inches and a stout Saxon, high, stout made, very upright and had on a black cloak.

FIRST HIGHWAYMAN: N.B. One of the men had a quantity of pimples on his face.

SECOND HIGHWAYMAN: And the other had his right eye blood shot.

FIRST HIGHWAYMAN: And appeared in the dress like gentleman's servants.

SECOND HIGHWAYMAN: Whoever will give information, whereby the offenders may be brought to justice shall, on conviction, receive a reward of fifty pounds.

THEY ROAR WITH LAUGHTER AND RUSH OFF.

COACH DRIVER HONKS DERISIVELY AT RETREATING HIGHWAYMEN.

ALL SING (MOVING CHAIRS AND STOOLS AS THEY MOVE TO EXITS): He that will not merry, merry be,
With a company of jolly boys,
May he be plagued with a scolding wife,
To confound him with her noise,
Let him be merry, merry, merry there,
And we will be merry, merry here;
For who can know where we may go
To be merry another year.

ALL GO OFF BUT THOSE FOR NEXT SCENE, A LADY AND MAID. TWO DANDIES ATTENTIVE TO LADY. LIGHTS BRIGHT AGAIN. LINKING MANDOLINE PHRASE.


## DANDIES SCENE

MAID: Coaches to run without horses, ma'am.

LADY: Mercy on us. In a short time, instead of travelling along in a comfortable coach, with a pair of beautiful stallions moving gracefully along the road, we may expect to hear a monster of a thing, travelling furiously along.

MAID: Fizzing, steaming and clattering, ma'am.
Leaving a trail of smoke behind it, ma'am.

LADY: Like one of Whiston's comets!

ALL LAUGH. MAID TOO LONG. SHE CURTSEYS
APOLOGETICALLY.

FIRST DANDY (LANGUID): Today we had a lark of
a very high order. Lady Wilton sent over to say
the locomotive machine was to be upon the railway at
such a place at twelve noon. I had the dissatisfaction,
for I cannot call it pleasure, of riding on it for five
miles at twenty miles per hour...the speed to me is
frightful; it gave me a headache, which has not left
me yet.

SECOND DANDY (VERY VAIN): I dislike railways because they cut up the country. I object to them because I object to anyone running across my property,
excepting myself. I have an especial aversion to
tunnels and cannot see upon what grounds England has
to be 'bored' by them, what!

HE LAUGHS. THEY LAUGH, ARTIFICIALLY.

In fact, if railways are allowed to run much longer,
England will soon be reduced to a state of ashes and
will have to be swept twice a year, or else ultimately
disappear from the surface of the globe.

FIRST DANDY: Have you heard...about the train that
left London and was never heard of again? And the
excursion train that took out five thousand children
and returned with one thousand, killed, wounded or
missing.

MAID: Ma'am!

LADY: Woe to them that come within the vortex of the
steam locomotive!

MANDOLINE PHRASE PLAYS THEM OFF AND THE
THREE COMMITTEE MEN ON. THEY WALK SLOWLY
ACROSS THE MAP ON THE STAGE AND SPEAK
PARTLY TO EACH OTHER AS THOUGH WORKING
OUT THE MINUTES, MOSTLY DIRECT TO THE
AUDIENCE.


## POTTERIES RAILWAY COMMITTEE

HEATHCOTE: At a meeting of manufacturers, tradesmen

and other inhabitants of the Staffordshire Potteries,
held at the Swan Inn, Hanley on Tuesday, the thirteenth
day of January eighteen thirty-five, Richard Edensor
Heathcote in the Chair –

ENOCH WOOD: It was resolved that, with a view to promote
the important interests of this manufacturing district,
it appears highly desirable that it should possess the
superior facilities and other advantages of transit for
its raw materials and productions, by means of a railway.

RIDGEWAY (GESTURING TOWARDS IT): That the proximity
of the Birmingham and Liverpool Railway seems most
opportune and affords the readiest mode for the attain-
ment of this object.

ENOCH WOOD (DESCRIBING IT ON THE MAP WITH HIS
STICK): That a line of road, forming the segment of a
circle extending from the north to the south, con-
necting at suitable and convenient distances with
longitudinal branches to the different towns, appears
the best way to subserve the whole of the district.

HEATHCOTE: That a committee be appointed to take into
consideration the propriety and advantage of con-
structing a branch, to communicate with the Liverpool
and Birmingham Railway – to report its sentiments
thereon – to receive subscriptions for defraying the
expense of a survey and estimate, and to ask Mr
George Stephenson, Civil Engineer, to make such
survey and report his opinion of the amount of capital
required.

THE ACTOR PLAYING RIDGEWAY GIVES HIS HAT
AND FROCK COAT TO ENOCH WOOD AND ROLLS
UP HIS SLEEVES. OTHERS GO OFF. HE IS NOW
GRANDAD, A YOUNG MAN IN COBBLER'S APRON.


## LEN PRESTON'S GRANDAD

LEN PRESTON (RECORDED VOICE OVER LOUDSPEAKER):
My grandfather helped to cut it from the bare turf
as a navvy. It so happened that he was a country
shoemaker (ENTER BOY WHO CROSSES TO
PRESTON) at Mavesyen Ridware, close to Rugeley,
in Staffordshire and the news came from the market by

farmers to the village that they were cutting what they called a new fangled railraod and they wanted hefty men who could use pick and shovel and they were paid every week for their wages.

THEY HAVE TURNED AS IF HEARING THE NEWS.

And as it so happened being a shoemaker in those days they were only paid once per year when they'd done the job. (GRANDAD SHOWS EMPTY POCKETS) So they'd got quite a big little family (ENTER WIFE AND TWO DAUGHTERS) which eventually got to eight boys and four girls. So he had it over with his young wife (GRANDAD TAKES WIFE ASIDE) as to whether he should treck across country and get a job and get some ready money. So she agreed to it (MANDOLINE PHRASE – HE TAKES OFF HIS APRON, KISSES FAMILY, THEY GO OFF) and he packed his bundle and trekked across country to the contractors and of course, being a hefty young chap, he got started as a navvy.

ENGINEER ENTERS AND GIVES GRANDAD A PICK AND SHOVEL. GRANDAD TAKES OUT A NEWS-PAPER AND READS. A NAVVY CLEANS A SHOVEL NEARBY.

And it so happened that, one day, he was reading the old Staffordshire Advertiser. His wife, by some means or other had got it conveyed to him and he was reading this newspaper and one of the engineers happened to see him reading it, which was a most unusual thing in those days, which is about and hundred and twenty-eight years ago, that is for a working man to be able to read or write.

ENGINEER: Are you reading that?

GRANDAD: Aye.

ENGINEER: What, proper reading?

GRANDAD: Aye.

ENGINEER: Can'st read then?

GRANDAD: Aye, and do numbers what I taught myself.

LEN PRESTON (RECORDED): Anyway, the engineer took him into the office and tested him to see what he could do. And he found as he could read and write and do figures. So he yanked him out of the gang and made him into a surveyor's chain man (ENGINEER GIVES GRANDAD A SURVEYOR'S POLE) and he stayed at the particular job then until the end. And eventually when the railway was opened he got a job as Station Master at Dove Bank, Uttoxeter.

## STEPHENSON SCENE

BANJO INTRODUCTION TO GEORDIE STEPHENSON SONG.

LOUDSPEAKER ANNOUNCEMENT: George Stephenson makes a survey of the proposed Potteries Railway.

ENTER STEPHENSON AND ENGINEER, NOW WITH SURVEYORS' INSTRUMENT ON A TRIPOD. THROUGH-OUT THE SCENE STEPHENSON DIRECTS ENGINEER (AND GRANDAD WITH POLE) TO DIFFERENT POINTS ON THE STAGE TO TAKE READINGS.

JEFF AND ANNE SING (UNACCOMPANIED): He came from up the Tyne, Geordie Stephenson,
A place called Wylam, Geordie Stephenson,
He went straight down the mine,
Like the others of his time,
But he had to make a line,
Geordie Stephenson.

STEPHENSON (ALWAYS TO AUDIENCE IN THIS SCENE):
My senses are puzzled in judging how these people can set about making such paltry objections! Is the great throughfare through England and Scotland to be turned aside injuriously for the frivolous remarks made by Lord Howick? Are hundreds and thousands of people to be turned through a tunnel just to please two or three individuals? No! The times are changed. The legislators must look to the comforts and con-veniences of the public.

BANJO CHORD.

JEFF AND ANNE: He was a man from up the street, Geordie Stephenson,
A man that you could meet, Geordie Stephenson,
Up Newcastle he would gang
When he thought himself a plan,

'Cos he was a thinking man,
Geordie Stephenson.

STEPHENSON: The strength of Britain lies in her iron
and coal beds; and the locomotive is destined, above
all other agencies, to bring it forth. The Lord Chancellor now sits upon a bag of wool; but wool has long
ceased to be emblematical of the staple commodity of
England. He ought rather to sit upon a bag of coals.

BANJO CHORD.

SINGERS: You've heard of Rocket's fame, Geordie
Stephenson,
It was that as made his name, Geordie Stephenson,
It ran from Liverpool,
Why the lad he was no fool,
And at twelve he left his school,
Geordie Stephenson.

BANJO PLAYS TUNE OF SONG QUIETLY THROUGH
NEXT SPEECH

STEPHENSON: I will tell you that I think you will live to
see the day, though I may not live so long, when the
railways will come to supercede almost all other
methods of conveyance in this country – when mail
coaches will go by railway, and railroads will become
the great highway for the King and all his subjects.
The time is coming when it will be cheaper for a
working man to travel upon a railway than to walk on
foot. I know there are great and almost insurmountable
difficulties to be encountered; but what I have said
will come to pass as sure as you live.

BANJO CHORD ENDS TUNE.

SINGERS: He was the King of Steam, Geordie Stephenson,
And he worked a simple scheme, Geordie Stephenson,
And that was 'Persevere'
And the critics never fear,
It's the envious that jeer,
Geordie Stephenson.

STEPHENSON: I am now called George Stephenson, Esq.,
of Tapton House, Near Chesterfield. I have dined
with Princes, Peers and commoners, with persons
of all classes, from the humblest to the highest. I
have also dined off a red herring in the hedge bottom

and I have gone through immense drudgery, and the conclusion I have come to is this; when we are all stripped, there is not much difference.

BANJO CHORD.

SINGERS (NOW WITH GILLIAN): We could go on all day, Geordie Stephenson,
But we've had our little say, Geordie Stephenson,
You've left a thousand signs,
On the track and down the mine,
And we reckon you did fine,
Geordie Stephenson.

## STEPHENSON'S REPORT

HEATHCOTE, ENOCH WOOD AND RIDGEWAY ENTER TO STEPHENSON WHO HANDS HEATHCOTE A COPY OF THE REPORT AND CONDUCTS THEM OVER THE MAP WHICH FORMS THE STAGE CLOTH TO DEMON-STRATE HIS POINTS.

STEPHENSON: Twenty fifth of August, eighteen thirty-five. Report by Mr George Stephenson on the proposed railway from the Potteries to the Grand Junction Railway. Gentlemen, in compliance with your request I have now to lay before you my report upon the route and direction of the branch railway proposed to connect the manufacturing districts of Stoke upon Trent, Etruria, Longport, Hanley, Lane End and the other contiguous manufactures with the Grand Junction Railway.

THEY MOVE UP TO THE HEAD OF THE VALLEY AND STAND ALONGSIDE STEPHENSON.

In thus examining the country I have fully satisfied myself that no line can be adopted to be so convenient and cheap, both in foundation and working, as that down the valley of the Trent – I therefore recommend taking the levels near to the south end of the tunnel at Harecastle, continuing down the valley (THEY MOVE OFF) nearly parallel to Fowlea Brook, till arriving at Stoke upon Trent. From this place the general direction of the Grand Trunk Canal would be taken to within a short distance of Stone, where it is proposed that the line should diverge westward, across the valley of the Trent and join the Grand Junction Railway near Norton Bridge.

STEPHENSON HANDS OUT THE ESTIMATE.

The above route pointed out to you is, on the whole, very favourable, as is shown by the estimate, and I do not see that any just opposition can be raised against it by any of the landowners. The only persons that appear to me to have any grounds for claiming damages are the owners of Whieldon Grove at Stoke and the Earl of St Vincent at Meaford. In the latter case the line can be so managed as to be quite out of sight from the house.

HEATHCOTE: Good, good.

STEPHENSON: The total length of the railway from Norton to Near Harecastle is about fourteen miles, on no part of which the inclinations exceed sixteen feet per mile, and that is a descent in favour of the load in passing down from the Potteries.

MURMURS OF APPROVAL FROM THE MANUFAC-TURERS.

My advice to you in forming this branch is this: to buy land and build bridges for a double line of railway but, in the first instance, to lay a single one only, as I imagine that two powerful engines will do all the business, both of passengers and goods of heavy merchandise, that you can require at first but, should the traffic turn out so great as to render a single way insufficient, you would then be well able to lay down the second one, having the land purchased and the bridges of sufficient dimensions for that purpose.

STEPHENSON MOVES ACROSS TO THE NEWCASTLE SIDE AND THEY FOLLOW. HE DEMONSTRATES TUNNEL LENGTH AND HEIGHT WITH HIS STICK.

Towards Apedale I have not taken any levels, as it has struck me that a communication could be effected with that coal field at a much less cost by driving a tunnel, which need be only six feet wide and six feet high, from Etruria to Mr Heathcote's canal, just before it reaches Newcastle. It appears that this branch, a mile and a half long, with a tunnel of about a mile, might be made for ten thousand pounds.

The waggons would be worked through the tunnel by a small stationary engine at the upper end. This scheme is the cheapest mode of effecting a junction with the Newcastle Coal Basin.

Now, the sum that I consider necessary for the formation of the main line is a hundred and forty thousand pounds for a double way, or a hundred and six thousand pounds for a single way – as above explained to you. The items are as follows:

HE PASSES ESTIMATE TO HEATHCOTE.

HEATHCOTE: Double line – cuttings and embankments: Seven hundred thousand cubic yards at one shilling a yard...thirty–five thousand pounds. Bridges, culverts, masonry etc...thirteen thousand five hundred and seventy pounds. Rails, chairs, keys, pins etc...thirty–four thousand three hundred and twenty pounds. Blocks and sleepers...fifteen thousand eight hundred and forty pounds. Fencing and gates...four thousand three hundred and twelve pounds. Laying and ballasting the way...ten thousand five hundred and sixty pounds. Land...fourteen thousand pounds. Giving a grand total, which includes contingencies, of...one hundred and forty thousand pounds.

STEPHENSON: In forming the above estimate, I have allowed liberally for every item that can be required in the execution of the railway. For example, for the land I have estimated an average of eight acres per mile at a hundred pounds an acre. The rails are estimated to be fifty shillings per yard and, from Stoke upon Trent, the line may be taken along either side of the canal without materially increasing the expense of that portion of the line. I am, gentlemen, your most obedient servant, George Stephenson.

HE GOES OFF. GUITAR ACCOMPANIMENT TO SONG BEGINS. THE TWO GIRLS COME FORWARD WATCHED BY THE ACTORS WHO PLAYED WOOD AND RIDGEWAY, WHO BEGIN TO CHANGE FOR THEIR NEXT CHARACTERS. LIGHTING DIMS A LITTLE.

## TOWNS UPON A HILL

GILLIAN AND ANNE SING WITH GUITAR: Hanley and
    Burslem were towns upon a hill,
  Fowlea Brook ran down from Goldenhill,
  And the valley it was green
  And the hills they were serene,
  But the coming of machine
  Takes the life from out the green
  And the coming of the rail
  Will drive the deadly nail
  In the coffin of the day
  When the green turns into grey.
  Hanley and Burslem were towns upon a hill.

  Viewed down from Tunstall was a valley low and wide,
  From Kidsgrove to Fenton grass on every side.
  Down Fowlea it is true, the willow trees all grew
  But the trains come rushing by
  The disease will multiply
  And factories by the score,
  Like an awful running sore,
  And the piercing of the track
  Will make our green lands black.
  Viewed down from Tunstall was a valley low and wide.

THUNDER, LIGHTNING. STAGE DARKENS.

## OAK FARM SCENE

ENTER NARRATOR, IN LONG BLACK CLOAK. HE
ORATES GRANDLY AND SWEEPS ABOUT THE STAGE.

NARRATOR: We'll tell you a tale of days gone by,
  When the rail was just beginning,
  How a countryman was robbed of his land
  By a lawyer's crafty conniving.

  'Twas in the eighteen-forties
  Across from Stoke to Dee,
  Rode a man from Nantwich,
  A crafty lawyer he.

  It was a wild and stormy night,
  That thus my story doth unfold,
  A rainy, howling, windy night,
  A stormy night – and cold.

He knew of all the railway plans,
He'd read them in the news sheet,
And in his mind he visualised
The place the tracks would meet.

ENTER FARMER AND WIFE, DRESSED IN COUNTRY
SMOCKS. NARRATOR BECOMES VILLAIN.

VILLAIN: Ha ha, ha ha, what do I see,
Is this the very place?
A broken down farm in the midst of a bog,
Now to show me face.

If I can once secure this land,
My ambition will come true.
For I foresee the future site
Of a station, known as Crewe.

HE LAUGHS. FARMER AND WIFE COME TO CENTRE
OF STAGE.

FARMER: We are poor country people,
I've been farming all my life.
I live here in a wilderness
With two pigs and the wife.

WIFE: Our home is near in ruins,
It's all that we have got.
Some marshy fields, a pair of pigs
And a cottage with dry rot.

We've got the clothes we stand in,
We work from dusk to dawn
And nature's very cruel
Just listen to that storm.

FARMER: Be raining hard,

WIFE:                  it be.

FARMER: Be draughty too,

WIFE:                  it are.

FARMER: If only we 'ad some money

WIFE: A sorry plight we are.

VILLAIN CREEPS TOWARDS THEM AND MAKES A
KNOCKING GESTURE.

VILLAIN: Knock knock.

FARMER: Hark!

WIFE: Hark! A knock this time of night,
Whoever can it be?

FARMER: There's only one way to find out,
Open the door and see.

FARMER MAKES MIME OF OPENING DOOR
WITH CREAKS.

VILLAIN: Dear friends, me 'umblest greetings,
My word you're looking well.
I've taken a fancy to this farm,
How would you like to sell?

HE CHINKS MONEY BAG.

It strikes me as a nice place.
(ASIDE): It's really a broken-down dump,
Ideal for me retirement.
(ASIDE): Not even a water pump.

For the cowshed I'll give you a fiver,
I can't be more generous than that,
(ASIDE): The Grand Junction line to Manchester
Will rise gleaming out of that.

For the back field a magnificent offer,
Thirty five pounds to you,
(ASIDE): Poor simple deluded wretches,
They don't know it's going to be Crewe.

Now what do you say to my offer?
A generous one, I'm not mean.
Come, come now, give me your answer.

FARMER: All right done.

VILLAIN (GIVES MONEY BAG): Ha, ha, you have been!

Now out into the stormy night
You go, with wife and goods.
And if you've got nowhere to go
You can sleep out in my woods.

WIFE (THEY GO AWAY TOWARDS AN EXIT): Alas,
alack, what shall we do?
This is a sorry plight.
We've got some cash but nowhere to go
On this wild and stormy night.

VILLAIN (LEAPS ABOUT): I've won, I've won, the deed
    is done,
  Ha, ha the die is cast.
  O'er this rich land the rail will run,
  I've made me fortune at last.

NARRATOR (NOW AS HIMSELF): He jumped for joy,
    began to sing,
  And he danced upon the spot.
  Which was a rather foolish thing,
  For the cottage had dry rot.

  His villainy was hard to believe,
  He cared for no man's plight.
  His ambition rode o'er all obstacles,
  A foul deed was done that night.

FARMER: Suddenly, a youth appeared.

  YOUTH ENTERS IN FRILLY WHITE SHIRT AND
  CARRYING A ROSE.

  The conscience of the nation.
  To condemn this rape upon the land
  And the evils of speculation.

  A gentle youth, a pretty youth,
  With chubby, dimpled cheek,
  A flower clasped in his loving hand,
  He opened his mouth to speak:

YOUTH: Ah woe, ah woe, for England green,
  Encroached upon by vile machine.
  I weep for thee, I shed a tear,
  That e'er vile rail should trespass here.

  To progress we must all submit,
  A sorry state, I must admit,
  To think that from this vile transaction
  Shall arise the glories of Crewe Junction.

NARRATOR (SUITING ALL ACTIONS TO HIS WORDS):
  Our villain raised a beady eye,
  And fixed him with a glare,

VILLAIN: I care not for your morals, youth,
  I'm rich now, I don't care.

NARRATOR: He cast the youth's ideals aside,
  Scorning his words so sweet.

The lad just stood and bitterly cried,
His flower lay crushed at his feet.

TABLEAU. INSTRUMENTAL ACCOMPANIMENT TO
SPECULATION SONG BEGINS (ON BANJO, GUITAR
AND ACCORDION). THE WHOLE CAST ASSEMBLE ON
OR ROUND THE MUSICIANS' ROSTRUM WITH FOUR
MEN IN THE CENTRE, BACK TO BACK, HOLDING
RED WHITE AND BLACK SURVEYORS POLES. THE
ACCOMPANIMENT LASTS THROUGHOUT THE SCENE,
VARYING ACCORDING TO THE DEVELOPING ACTION.

SURVEYORS' POLE DANCE AND SONG

ALL SING: If you want to make a fortune, I'll tell you
    what to do,
    We want to make a railway line from Derby up to
        Crewe,
    But how we're going to build it, we haven't got a
        clue,
    For our only interest is speculation.

AS THE POLEMEN SPEAK (TO AUDIENCE) THEY
MOVE OUT TO OPPOSITE CORNERS OF THE STAGE.

FIRST POLEMAN (WHO PLAYED GEORGE STEPHENSON):
The middle years of the eighteen-forties were the
period of Railway Mania.

SECOND POLEMAN: A reckless spirit of gambling set in,
which completely changed the character of railway
enterprise.

THIRD POLEMAN: Many persons, utterly ignorant of
railways, rushed eagerly into the vortex, hungering
and thirsting after the profit they might gain,

LOUDSPEAKER ANNOUNCEMENT: Twenty-four railway
companies are set up to promote twenty-four separate
railway lines through North Staffordshire.

THE DANCE NOW BEGINS. THE POLEMEN IN A KIND
OF POKER FACED LOPING JOG TROT MOVE ACROSS
THE MAP AS THEY SPEAK, IN THEIR VARIOUS
ROUTES. WHEN THEY ARRIVE, THEY MARK TIME.

POLE DANCE

FIRST POLEMAN: Birmingham, Lichfield and Uttoxeter Line.

SECOND POLEMAN: Buxton, Macclesfield and Congleton Line.

FOURTH POLEMAN: Congleton, Buxton and Crewe Line.

THIRD POLEMAN (ALWAYS WITH A KIND OF LONG BUT PANICKY STRIDE): Manchester, Congleton, Newcastle and Stone Line.

FIRST POLEMAN: Direct London to Manchester

SECOND POLEMAN: Direct Independent Manchester to London.

MEETS FIRST

FOURTH POLEMAN (PARTS FIRST AND SECOND): Leicester, Tean and Dove.

THIRD POLEMAN: Rugby, Burton, Ashbourne and Leek.

SECOND POLEMAN: Lichfield, Cheadle, Macclesfield.

FOURTH POLEMAN: Leek, Manchester, Macclesfield.

THIRD POLEMAN: Rugby, Derby, Macclesfield.

FIRST POLEMAN: North Staffordshire Railway Company.

FIRST POLEMAN ADVANCES ON THE OTHER THREE AS HE SPEAKS, THEY ALL JOG UP AND DOWN DISCOMFITEDLY IN MACCLESFIELD.

REST OF CAST SING WHILE FIRST POLEMAN DRIVES OTHER THREE BACKWARDS THEN IS DRIVEN BACK BY THEM: If you want to make a fortune, I'll tell you what to do,
We want to make a railway line from Derby up to Crewe,
But how we're going to build it, we haven't got a clue,
For our only interest is speculation

AFTER A MIMED CONSULTATION SECOND, THIRD AND FOURTH POLEMAN RETREAT TO CORNERS LEAVING ONE IN THE CENTRE. AS THEY SPEAK. THEY LOWER THEIR POLES LIKE LANCES.

SECOND POLEMAN: The London and Birmingham Railway
Company.

FOURTH POLEMAN: The Manchester and Birmingham
Railway Company.

THIRD POLEMAN: The Grand Junction Railway Company.

INSTRUMENTAL & DANCE:

> THEY CHARGE THE FIRST POLEMAN SIMULTAN-
> EOUSLY. HE NARROWLY AVOIDS SKEWERING.
> THEY FORM UP IN A LINE AND ADVANCE ON HIM
> TO A MENACING DRUM BEAT. HE SHUDDERS. THEY
> QUARREL, BONGING EACH OTHER WITH THEIR
> POLES AT THE LAST MOMENT AND STAGGER OFF
> DIZZILY LEAVING THE FIRST POLEMAN TRIU-
> MPHANT.

REST SING WHILE THE FIRST POLEMAN COMES TO
CENTRE HOLDING ALOFT HIS POLE: If you want to
make a fortune I'll tell you what to do,
We want to make a railway line from Derby up to
Crewe,
But how we're going to build it, we haven't got a clue
For our only interest is speculation.

> SONG ACCOMPANIMENT ENDS. PAUSE. BANJO
> PLAYS 'GEORGE STEPHENSON' SONG WHILE FIRST
> POLEMAN MARKS OUT RAILWAY ROUTE WITH HIS
> POLE.

LOUDSPEAKER ANNOUNCEMENT: eighteen forty-five.
The North Staffordshire Company's line is sanctioned
by Parliament – laid out along the line proposed by
George Stephenson. Macclesfield; to Kidsgrove Cen-
tral; to Longport; to Etruria; to Stoke-on-Trent; to
Barlaston; to Stone; to Norton Bridge.

> BANJO ENDS. PAUSE. ENTER SIR CHARLES
> WOLSELEY WITH CHAIR.

The country gentleman opposes the railway: Sir Charles
Wolseley, Bart. versus Enoch Wood, pot manufacturer.

WOLSELEY V. WOOD

ENTER MAID WITH ENOCH WOOD JR. HE PUTS A CHAIR DOWN.

MAID: Sir Charles, Mr Enoch Wood Junior is here to see you.

SIR CHARLES: Oh, show him in.

WOOD COMES FORWARD.

WOOD: Good evening, Sir Charles. I must apologise for this unexpected visit, but I have just read this letter in the Staffordshire Advertiser of the twenty-first of April from which I quote the following passage: 'On the twenty-third of February, whilst engaged in the checking the reference of the intended line of railway, a surveyor and myself were met by the solicitor of Sir Charles Wolseley, who gave us notice that, in case we set a foot on the land of Sir Charles Wolseley, we should immediately be taken into custody, as all Sir Charles Wolseley's servants were out upon the watch for us.'

MAID: Excuse me, sir...

WOOD: 'When we arrived at Grendon we were followed the whole day by a constable and a gamekeeper with a double barrelled gun, the latter of whom, whenever we made an enquiry from any person, stepped up to him, and desired in one instance to know what he, the passer-by, had to do with it. During the latter part of the day, we could not ask a question except in a whisper, that the constable could not overhear, so closely did he follow us and, on being remonstrated with, he became very abusive and impertinent.'

Sir Charles, I would like an explanation of these actions.

WOLSELEY (TO MAID): You may bring in the tea. (MAID GOES OFF.) Mr Wood, I see no reason why I should account to you for my actions. However, it is clear to me from that person's style and language it would appear that it is actually a crime for a Gentleman to defend his property from invasion! – a sort of minor treason not to permit engineers and surveyors to take surveys and make plans of his estate – to break down his fences, to remove his ancient landmarks and erect their own instead!

MAID RE-ENTERS WITH COOK BEARING A TEA TRAY
WITH A WOOD'S TEA SERVICE ON IT.

WOOD: Sir Charles, may I reiterate that we have always
made the utmost endeavours to avoid all molestation to
noblemen and gentlemens' seats, near which the
proposed line is intended to pass. The Railway Compay
has given direction to the surveyors to spare no expense
for this purpose. It is always ready and happy to communicate with all parties who wish an alteration in the
line. Sir Charles, there was no reason for such an
action as described in this letter.

MAID: Tea, Sir Charles.

SIR CHARLES: Thank you. Mr Wood, these persons are
trespassers. May I assert, without fear of contradiction,
that, by the law of England, all property and the
person of the humblest individual is sacred; that,
neither the room in which we are standing, nor my
lands and tenements, can be wrested from me by any
individual, or company of individuals. I have as much
right to what I enjoy as Queen Victoria has to the
Crown of these Realms. If it be absolutely necessary
to take any part of my property for the erection of even
barracks in time of war, or as a harbour for the de-
fence of the country, I must surrender it.

A case of absolute necessity must, however, be
made out before Parliament, The Queen, Lords and
Commons can, by force of an Act, deprive me of my
patrimonial estates.

WOOD: Sir Charles, may I remind you that on your family
crest are emblazoned the words: 'The greatest amount
of good to the greatest number'? And may I also remind you, Sir Charles, Mr Richard Edensor Heathcote, one of the largest landowners of the district, is
also the Chairman of the Potteries Railway Committee
and has realised that advantage to a private person
weighs less heavy in the balance than disadvantage
to the common good.

MAID: Tea, sir.

WOOD: Thank you.

MAID: Milk and sugar?

WOOD: Milk, please.

SIR CHARLES: Heathcote can do what he likes. As for myself, I intend to call upon all landowners to unite in resisting unnecessary inroads upon their estates for the sake of mere visionary speculations. Railways are as yet in their infancy. No one can say whether they will answer or no. All that is at present certain is that they have been the cause of a most unprecedented revolution in property and ruined thousands, while they have only enriched engineers and some few grasping attorneys.

WOOD: That is a blatant...

MAID HANDS TEA TO WOOD.

Thank you...Sir Charles, I, for one, feel no alarm that railway communications through the country would so multiply as to scare the nobility from the mansions of their fathers, or affright the gentry from the ancient houses of their families. (RAISES TEA CUP TO EYE LEVEL.) One of my own, I see. Sir Charles, I do not wish to tire you once again by reciting the benefits which a railway brings to a community. I would just like to point out one instance of this case. I refer to the Liverpool and Manchester Railway. Passengers are conveyed between Liverpool and Manchester in two hours for four and sixpence instead of in four to six hours by the stage coaches for ten or twelve shillings. Goods and merchandise of all kinds are conveyed from Liverpool to Manchester by the railway in four or five hours, for eleven shillings a ton, instead of from thirty-six hours to a week or ten days at fifteen shillings a ton, by the water conveyance.

Commodities get cheaper and cheaper. Who knows, one day even your servants may be able to afford my pottery. The most rapid coaches travel at the rate of nine or ten miles an hour, a speed which in three or four years destroys the horses, while the locomotive engines travel regularly from fifteen to twenty miles an hour, and occasionally with much greater rapidity.

SIR CHARLES: That may be. But the most which this railway in question can accomplish is to enable the

Manchester merchants and cotton spinners to arrive
in London half an hour earlier than by the present
line of railway; and perhaps, also, Doll Draggle-
Tail of Billingsgate may get her smock made half an
hour sooner! But are these cases so pressing and
urgent as to justify Parliament in depriving me and
other dissenting landowners of our lands and tenements and driving us by the intolerable nuisances
which every railway brings with it, from our ancient
family residences? Am I, and other individuals
proposed to be sacrificed, not a part of the public?
And are we not the Queen's subjects and as much
entitled to protection as the inhabitants of Manchester?

WOOD: Sir Charles, do you suppose that that is a full
and fair statement of the case? Has the fact escaped
your notice that the saving of half an hour would
accommodate thousands who might be expected to
pass daily along the line? The whole population of
Manchester and the surrounding towns in Lancashire,
the inhabitants of Stockport, Macclesfield, Congleton
and the Potteries, heartily concurred in the project,
from the conviction that they would be essentially
benefited by it; for though you, Sir Charles, from
your secluded habits, seem not to be aware that the
saving of time and money to thousands and tens of
thousands actively employed in trade and commerce,
is an object of public importance, they are fully
aware of it. Good day.

HE GOES OFF. GUITAR BEGINS INSTRUMENTAL
TO NEXT SONG.

LOUDSPEAKER ANNOUNCEMENT: Parliament over-
rides the landowner's objections. The railway lines
are to be laid.

ALL CAST ENTER DURING FOLLOWING SONG.
EACH VERSE IS SUNG BY MORE AND MORE MEN,
WITH THE GIRLS HUMMING AND THEN JOINING IN
THE CHORUS. ALL ARE NOW DRESSED AS NAVVIES.

## PADDY WORKS ON THE RAILWAY

JEFF AND ONE NAVVY SING: In eighteen hundred and
forty-one

Me corduroy breeches I put on,
Me corduroy breeches I put on
To work upon the railway.

ALL SING: Filli-mi-ooree-ooree-ay,
Filli-mi-ooree-ooree-ay,
Filli-mi-ooree-ooreepay,
To work upon the railway.

JEFF AND TWO NAVVIES SING: In eighteen hundred and
forty-two
From Hartlepool I moved to Crewe
And found myself a job to do
A-working on the railway.

ALL SING: Filli-mi-ooree-ooree-ay,
Filli-mi-ooree-ooree-ay,
Filli-mi-ooree-ooree-ay,
To work upon the railway.

JEFF AND THREE NAVVIES SING: In eighteen hundred
and forty-three
I broke me shovel across me knee
And went to work for the company
On the Leeds and Selby Railway

ALL SING: Filli-mi-ooree-ooree-ay,
Filli-mi-ooree-ooree-ay,
Filli-mi-ooree-ooree-ay,
To work upon the railway.

JEFF AND FOUR NAVVIES SING: In eighteen hundred and
forty-four
I landed on the Liverpool shore,
Me belly was empty, me back was sore
From working on the railway.

ALL SING: Filli-mi-ooree-ooree-ay,
Filli-mi-ooree-ooree-ay,
Filli-mi-ooree-ooree-ay,
To work upon the railway.

JEFF AND ALL SING: In eighteen hundred and forty-
five
To go to Stoke I did contrive
To go to Stoke I did contrive
To work upon the railway.

ALL SING: Filli-mi-ooree-ooree-ay,
Filli-mi-ooree-ooree- ay,

Filli-mi-ooree-ooree-ay,
To work upon the railway.

SOUND OF BELLS RINGING

LOUDSPEAKER ANNOUNCEMENT: Twenty-third September eighteen forty-five — the first sod of the North
Staffordshire railway is cut.

BANJO PLAYS JAUNTY VERSION OF STEPHENSON
SONG THROUGHOUT THE FIRST PART OF THE
SCENE.


CUTTING THE FIRST SOD

AS THE NARRATOR DESCRIBES THE SCENE, THE
REST OF THE CAST MARCH UP AND DOWN IN A DEMON-
STRATION OF THE EVENTS.

NARRATOR: The day was observed as a general holiday,
throughout nearly the whole of the Potteries and Newcastle, business being suspended at the factories so
that the entire population could watch the cutting of
the first sod of the North Staffordshire Railway.

THE CROWD ASSEMBLE IN LINE OPPOSITE THE
NARRATOR.

The field in which the ceremony was to be performed
had for some time attracted a multitude of anxious
spectators.

THE CROWD MARCH IN LINE TOWARDS THE
NARRATOR.

None but those who had supplied themselves with
tickets, however, were permitted to enter the field...

THE CROWD BOO, ABOUT TURN AND MARCH BACK.

...and the crowd therefore were endeavouring as
good a view as possible from behind the hedges...

THE CROWD TRY TO SEE OVER THE HEDGE.

...Their curiosity at length became so much excited
that, despite attempts of the few policeman to restrain
them, they rushed through the gaps...

THE CROWD BREAK LINE AND MILL ABOUT THE
NARRATOR, THEN FORM SEMICIRCLE.

...at different points and surrounded the enclosure, so that the leading ceremony of the day – the cutting of the sod – was performed under circumstances of considerable confusion.

BANJO STOPS. THE CROWD PERFORM AN UNKIND VERSION OF CEREMONY WITH RIDICULOUS VOICES.

FIRST LAD: Mr Sharp, the Deputy Chairman, then presented the spade to Mr Ricardo. Spade.

RICARDO LAD: Hahoo!

RICARDO LAD MAKES GIBBERISH SPEECH

NARRATOR: In a few observations which were inaudible to all, excepting to about half a dozen persons immediately surrounding him, we understood him to declare that the North Staffordshire Railway would prove one of the most remunerative, as it would be one of the most important, lines in the kingdom.

COPELAND LAD (FAT WALK): Mr Alderman Copeland presented the barrow, addressing a few remarks to Mr Ricardo. Barrow.

RICARDO LAD: Hahoo!

ANOTHER LAD: Mr Ricardo, in accepting the implements, addressed a few spirited and good humoured remarks to those who could hear him.

RICARDO LAD (GIBBERS): I would like one sod to stand on, and another to cut.

NARRATOR: The honourable gentleman then proceeded to handle the ceremonial instrument.

RICARDO LAD MIMES PREPARATION THEN BENDING OF SPADE. CROWD GROANS.

WOMAN: He's broken the bloody spade!

NARRATOR: Though so beautiful in appearance, it was not calculated for rough usage, and the first thrust of the honourable gentleman's foot fairly doubled it up and it was with some difficulty that the first sod was cut and lifted to the barrow.

RICARDO LAD MIMES RIPPING UP THE SOD AND THROWING IT IN THE BARROW. SOUND OF CANNON FIRING THREE SHOTS. THE CROWD SALUTE AND

SING GIBBERISH VERSION OF NATIONAL ANTHEM.

NARRATOR: Many persons appearing anxious to congratulate Mr Ricardo –

THE CROWD GO WITH HANDS OUTSTRETCHED TO RICARDO LAD.

– the honourable gentleman mounted a horse...and rode amongst the crowd...

RICARDO LAD MIMES LEAPING ON HORSE. THE CROWD LIFT UP ARMS TO HORSEMAN HEIGHT AND FOLLOW HIM.

...shouldering his spade.

OTHER LAD: And having lost his hat it was replaced by a new tommy hat, which one of the navvies happened luckily to have in his pocket.

GIVES HAT TO RICARDO LAD. THE CROWD CHEERS.

WOMEN: Navvies!

SILENCE.

WOMAN: So those are the navvies!

THE NAVVIES MOVE TO THE CENTRE AS MANDO-LINE ACCOMPANIMENT TO NAVVY SONG BEGINS. LIGHTS FADE TILL THERE IS ONLY A SMALL POOL IN THE CENTRE AND FOUR SHAFTS OF LIGHT PICKING OUT THE WOMEN AND A TOP HATTED GENT HIGH ABOVE THEM IN THE SURROUNDING AUDITORIUM GANGWAYS.


NAVVY SEQUENCE

LOUDSPEAKER ANNOUNCEMENT: Over the next two months two thousand railway navvies assembled to cut the line from Norton Bridge to Harecastle Tunnel.

MANDOLINE ENDS.

FIRST WOMAN: Their huts and houses are dens of the most appalling infamy.

SECOND WOMAN: The curse of a God-fearing and respectable district.

FIRST WOMAN: Dangerous beasts of prey.

SECOND WOMAN: Open shirts revealing hairy chests.

THIRD WOMAN: The manners of the navvies are such that we cannot even look at them without blushing.

TOP-HATTED GENTLEMAN: These banditti, known in some parts of England by the name of navvies or navigators and in others by that of bankers, are generally the terror of the surrounding country. They are in a particular class by themselves, as the gypsies; possess all the daring recklessness of the smuggler, without any of his redeeming qualities.

SECOND WOMAN: Their ferocious behaviour can only be equalled by the brutality of their language.

THIRD WOMAN: Their hand is against every man and, before you have been long acquainted, every man's hand is against them.

FIRST WOMAN: And woe befall any woman with the slightest share of modesty whose ears they can assail.

SECOND WOMAN: Thomas Appleby, railway labourer, was fined two pounds six shillings costs, or to undergo fourteen days hard labour for assaulting a Police Officer, whilst drunk, in Burslem Churchyard, on a Sunday afternoon.

THIRD WOMAN: Disturbing the peace of the neighbourhood.

SECOND WOMAN: Selling ale without a licence.

THIRD WOMAN: Drunken brawls.

SECOND WOMAN: Violence and robbery.

THIRD WOMAN: Breaking windows.

SECOND WOMAN: Daring ruffians.

THIRD WOMAN: Villainous looking rogues.

WOMEN'S LIGHTS FADE. MANDOLINE ACCOMPANIMENT BEGINS. WOMEN ACCOMPANY ON A CONTINUOUS DRONE.


NAVVY SONG

NAVVIES SING: You can sing of your soldiers and sailors,

Of the heroes who follow the drum,
But for great feats of might and of daring.
A new race of giants has come.
They call us the bold navigators,
Hard drinking, hard fighting and strong,
There are no finer boys in the nation,
And I'll tell of the deeds that we've done.

We waded through bog and through swampland,
Across valleys and rivers we strode,
We burrowed like moles in the ground, boys,
Moved mountains and hills by the load.
We dug Olive Mount's famous cutting,
Then across the great bog of Chat Moss,
There was nothing could stop the bold navvies,
And many a brave comrade we lost.

We bored the great Harecastle Tunnel,
Dug a hole under Liverpool town,
Saw our mates crushed to death under Woodhead
On that job of great fame and renown.
We lived on good beef and strong ale, boys,
And our home it was old Batty Green,
Far away from our wives and our families,
And the tracks mark the places we've been.

You can sing of your soldiers and sailors,
Of the heroes who follow the drum,
But for great feats of might and of daring,
A new race of giants has come.
They call us the bold navigators,
Hard drinking, hard fighting and strong,
There are no finer boys in the nation,
And I'll tell of the deeds that we've done.

SONG ENDS. TWO ECHOING THUDS LIKE A
PICKAXE IN A TUNNEL. A MOÚTH ORGAN
ALWAYS PLAYS JAUNTILY DURING ANNOUNCE-
MENTS.

LOUDSPEAKER ANNOUNCEMENT: Macclesfield Contract. Seven principal cuttings commenced, eighty
thousand cubic yards of earth removed. Clay ex-
cavated for forty million bricks for Harecastle
Tunnel and Congleton Viaduct.

Joseph Gillhall, Banksman, Number Seven Shaft,
Harecastle Tunnel, killed after falling a hundred and

fifty-six feet.

TWO THUDS. MOUTH ORGAN STOPS.

FIRST NAVVY (TO AUDIENCE – STEPPING OUT OF CENTRE GROUP, THE REST CROUCH LEANING ON PICKS OR SHOVELS): You want railways? Well, do you know what railways are? Railways are pick and shovel work, that's what they are. Chat Moss, Liverpool, you want to try pick and shovelling over bog. The Kilsby Tunnel, Liverpool and Birmingham Line, you want to try pick and shovelling over flooded workings.

Olive Mount, Liverpool, you want to try pick and shovelling through solid rock. For me, railways are pick and shovel work, Without us there'd be no railways. And I've come down here on railways – cuttings in Glasgow, embankments in Keswick, tunnels at Woodhead, and, aye, tunnels here at Harecastle. That's a long road with a pick and shovel.

SECOND NAVVY (STEPS FORWARD): I've been working in Harecastle Tunnel, what a rum place that is. It's dark, damp and smelling of stagnant water. The work is dangerous and thoroughly miserable, which makes us swear and mither about working double shifts. But then the money's good, I suppose. The only consolation is that we are not working up to our knees in water, like most tunnels we work in. This is on account of Brindley's canal, which is acting as a drainage for our tunnel. But the work is still dangerous. This mate of mine, Sam Williams, was working on coupling the waggons together, which we had loaded with clay and marl. While he was on the rails, three loaded waggons were being brought down to be attached and, seeing the danger we hollered out to him. The poor bastard didn't hear us, or was too confused to move out of the way, as he was smashed against the bumpers. After coughing up blood for an hour, we eventually freed him, then we took him home to his lodgings at Butt Lane.

Any road, there are plenty more good mates on the railway.

TWO THUDS. MOUTH ORGAN.

LOUDSPEAKER ANNOUNCEMENT: Great Haywood, twelve thousand yards of fencing erected. One thousand, three hundred and eighteen men and sixty-one horses now engaged. Cutting well forward. Samuel Williams, coupler, crushed between two waggons. Languished in his lodgings at Butt Lane several days, before he expired.

TWO THUDS. MOUTH ORGAN STOPS. YOUNG NAVVY STEPS FORWARD. ON THE OTHER SIDE OF THE CENTRE GROUP, BACKLIT SO THAT WE CANNOT SEE HER FACE, SEEMINGLY FAR AWAY AND NOT FACING HIM, A YOUNG WOMAN.

YOUNG NAVVY: Sometimes, I think of home.

WIFE: Come home.

YOUNG NAVVY: The mine shut down.

WIFE: There are other mines.

YOUNG NAVVY: There's no money down the mine.

WIFE: Come home.

YOUNG NAVVY: There's freedom on the railways. If I don't want to stay, I jack it in and work for another company. That way, I'm my own master.

WIFE: Your wife wants you home.

YOUNG NAVVY: I send you money. I never touch the drink. I never look on other women.

WIFE: We want you home. Come home.

TWO THUDS. MOUTH ORGAN. LIGHTS FADE ON THEM BOTH. CENTRE GROUP CROUCHES STILL.

LOUDSPEAKER ANNOUNCEMENT: Stoke/Uttoxeter Contract. Seven culverts are completed. Sixty-one thousand yards of excavation removed. Twenty-eight thousand yards of lineal fencing erected. Six hundred men, a hundred horses, four waggons and four hundred and seventy barrows now in use on the works. The accidents to workmen employed in the construction of the Churnet Valley Line have been numerous but amputations have been performed by Mr Heaton, Surgeon of Leek, with great skill and indefatigable attention to the sufferers.

TWO SHARP ECHOING THUDS. MOUTH ORGAN ENDS. VICAR ENTERS AND APPROACHES THE GROUP.

THIRD NAVVY (STEPS FORWARD): Yes, I am an English navvy, but oh not an English sot,
>    I have run my pick through alcohol, in bottle, glass or pot.
>    And with the spade of abstinence, and all the power I can
>    I am spreading out a better road for every working man.
>
>    I am an English navvy and I tell my tale with glee,
>    Though thousands curl their lips in scorn and mock at chaps like me;
>    But round and round our kingly isle, on meadow, glen and hill
>    Ten thousand mighty monuments proclaim our strength and skill.

VICAR: What's your name, my man?

THIRD NAVVY: Jeremiah Cumm.

VICAR: Have you prayed much to God during the year?

CUMM: This policeman, William Cox, accused me of making trouble outside a grocer's shop in Longton.

VICAR: Have you read the Bible very often?

CUMM: And said he's execute his duty on me. I said 'If you execute your duty on me – I'll execute mine on you'.

SECOND NAVVY: And what did you do?

CUMM: I thumped him.

>    NAVVIES LAUGH.

VICAR: Have you been as often as you ought or at all to a place of worship?

CUMM: And after a bit, I said, 'Will you release me?' and he said, 'No.' and I said, 'Then I'll serve you out.'

VICAR: Have you or have you not made yourself like one of the beasts that perish by the sin of drunkenness?

CUMM: The magistrate said that I was drunk. And he said I was no use at all.

VICAR: Have you been a swearing man?

CUMM: And fined me six pounds, or two months hard
labour but I couldn't face two months hard labour
so I paid up all me savings.

VICAR: Sister! (TO A HARD LOOKING WOMAN WHO HAS
NOW JOINED THEM.) What about you? Has your life
been the life of a Christian woman?

NAVVIES LAUGH.

Perhaps you will be killed suddenly by a fall of
earth and a blasting of rock, by the crushing blow of
an engine, by a bruise which may fester and mortify
and poison the life blood. But, however it may be, or
however it may happen, let me ask you, are you ready
now? Shall you be ready to meet death?

GREAT ECHOING ROAR. MANDOLINE BEGINS
NAVVIES SONG AGAIN. NAVVIES HUM IT UNDER
ANNOUNCEMENT.

LOUDSPEAKER ANNOUNCEMENT: The directors of the
North Staffordshire Railway have voted unanimously
to consider the employment in a light capacity of men
who have been lamed by accident on the construction
of the line. At the opening the usual festivities are
to be dispensed with, in view of the prevalent distress among the working classes of the Potteries
District. The sum of two hundred and fifty pounds has
been granted instead for the relief of the poor.

SONG ENDS. LIGHTS FADE UP A LITTLE – A
GENERAL DISMAL LIGHT.


QUEUE SCENE

ENTER THREE WOMEN TO JOIN THE QUEUE AND A
SANDWICH BOARD MAN WHOSE BOARDS ANNOUNCE
THE OPENING OF THE RAILWAY. HE SEEMS TO BE A
SIMPLETON, OLD, BEWILDERED.

SANDWICH BOARD MAN: Railway Opening – Sensational
opening of railway!

FIRST WOMAN: Come on, Mother.

SECOND WOMAN: How long have you been here, love?

OLD WOMAN: I'm worn out.

SECOND WOMAN: Three hours! Did you hear that? Three hours!

OLD WOMAN: Where's the end of it then?

FIRST WOMAN: Up there.

SANDWICH BOARD MAN: Grand opening!...

THE QUEUE SLOWLY EASES FORWARD ACROSS THE STAGE. ENTER CHARITY WORKER. HE ADDRESSES THE QUEUE.

CHARITY WORKER: At this time of distress and unemployment of the working classes, we are gratified to be able to apply the generosity of the directors of the new North Staffordshire Railway to provide a soup distribution unit for this town, in its present great need.

SANDWICH BOARD MAN: Sensational opening!

CHARITY WORKER: Thank you....Excuse me.

OLD WOMAN: They're opening a railway.

FIRST WOMAN: Won't do us much good.

A ROUGH LOOKING MAN – A CHARTIST – COMES ON WITH A BOX FITTED UP AS A SMALL SPEAKING PLATFORM. HE GOES UP TO THE QUEUE.

CHARTIST: People of Stoke, I am a Chartist. And I invite you to a meeting behind the Brethren's Room in Hanley on Tuesday next. Come to it. It concerns you. It concerns a Charter, that we are demanding for the people, that the people might be represented in Parliament, that the people help govern this country, that the people represent the people.

SANDWICH BOARD MAN: Sensational Opening!...

THE CHARTIST STANDS UP ON HIS PLATFORM AND HARANGUES THE QUEUE

CHARTIST: The government of this country consists of a band of privileged banditti, working only to defend the wealth of the privileged classes. The House of Commons is an unenlightened, ignorant body, consisting of the most indolent, selfish, ignorant, bloody-minded set of men anywhere to be found.

OLD WOMAN: There's a man looking at you.

CHARTIST: Look at you this day, the opening of a railway, which should bring benefit and prosperity to the ordinary people. What is your part in it? Two hundred and fifty pounds worth of charity. Very generous, you might say but I say to you, the Secretary of the North Staffordshire Railway gets a salary of a thousand pounds a year. The children of Spittals Workhouse are getting a treat, tea and cakes. They appear to the generosity of the Directors of the North Staffordshire Railway, new pressed and starched in their Workhouse pinafores. I say, there should be no Workhouse pinafores, no Workhouse, if this country was governed by men of the working classes. The Pottery Towns are being allocated this day, charitably, the following items of food: three quarters of a hundredweight of tea; two hundredweight of lump sugar; eight hundred loaves of bread, two thousand buns and seventeen gallons of wine. A feast you might say. (THE TWO DANDIES FROM SECOND SCENE COME ON.) But I say to you, divide that among the population of the Potteries, and then compare it with what the Directors of the North Staffordshire Railway will eat at their banquet this evening and you will have a true picture of the comparative privileges of the ruling classes. Don't be blinded by charity, demand your rights.

HE STEPS DOWN AND SPREADS A FRENCH FLAG ON THE GROUND IN FRONT OF THEM.

I spread before you the Tricolour of the freedom-winning people of France. And now I call for three cheers for the French Republic, three cheers for the French Republic, three cheers for the Chartist Movement and a groan for the Government Sedition Bill. Hip hip!

FIRST DANDY: Three cheers for the North Staffordshire Railways, three cheers for the industry of the Potteries...

SECOND DANDY: – and one groan for the Chartist rebels.

THE CHARTIST GOES FOR THE DANDIES. ENTER CAVALRY OFFICER CARRYING GLASS OF PORT. THE CHARTIST GOES. ENTER THE CHARITY WORKER NERVOUSLY.

OFFICER: What's going on here?

CHARITY WORKER: Trouble?

OFFICER: There'll be no trouble.

CHARITY WORKER: The populace has been quite docile during their recent travails but, with this Chartist agitation, there could be a flare-up at any time.

OFFICER: There'll be no trouble. Our Regiment is here for a while yet.

CHARITY WORKER: They don't like it, I know. They say 'We don't want yeomen cavalry riding about our streets.' But the very fact of your NOT being needed is the best proof of the efficiency of your services, in my opinion.

OLD WOMAN (IN THE QUEUE): Lost something?

OFFICER: I beg your pardon?

OLD WOMAN: Where's your 'orse?

LAUGHTER. DISTANT SOUND OF WHISTLES, AND A STEAM ENGINE SLOWLY STARTING. CHEERS.

CHARITY WORKER: Good people, there is still an adequate supply of soup but we fear there is no more bread.

DISTANT TRAIN CHUFFS RHYTHMICALLY.

WOMEN: No bread, no bread, no bread.

BANJO ACCOMPANIMENT TO SONG BEGINS

LOUDSPEAKER ANNOUNCEMENT: Seventeenth of April, eighteen forty-eight – Railway Line opened from Stoke-on-Trent to the Grand Junction Railway at Norton Bridge.


HURRAH FOR STEAM

JEFF, GILLIAN, ANNE AND ALAN SING. THE LAST THREE ARE DRESSED UP FOR A POSH DINNER.

Come all you bold people and to me pay heed,
There's a new way of travelling at a very great speed,
Straight through the country, like a monster it seems,
An iron locomotive that's driven by steam.

THE REST OF THE CAST ENTER ALL DRESSED
UP AND GREET AS IF BEFORE A PUBLIC DINNER.
THERE ARE LADIES. WE NOTICE WOOD AND
HEATHCOTE. EVERYONE LOOKS VERY HAPPY.

ALL: They said twas impossible what has been done
By Richard Trevithick and George Stephenson,
They've built a strange horse that doesn't eat hay,
But runs upon wheels down the straight iron way.

Now the steam engine's here, the old times are past
Twenty-five miles per hour is recklessly fast
Hard luck to the highwayman, he'll lose his job
For a new railway train you never could rob.


BANQUET SCENE

ENOCH WOOD (TO COPELAND): Sir Charles Wolseley
reminds me of the fop in Shakespeare's HENRY IV,
who visited Hotspur on the battlefield and called
them 'Untaught knaves, unmannerly,
To bring a slovenly, unhandsome corpse (alias the
railway train)
Betwixt the wind and his nobility.'

ALL LAUGH.

HEATHCOTE: Gentlemen, at the time of the opening of
the Trent and Mersey Canal, the population of the
Pottery district was not more than ten thousand, but
the completion of that great undertaking gave such
an impetus to our trade that the Potteries soon became the principal seat of the earthenware manu-
facture and the population increased so rapdidly that
I believe it now numbers upwards of a hundred thousand. I trust and firmly believe that similar results
will follow the opening of the new North Staffordshire
Railway.

APPLAUSE. INSTRUMENTAL PLAYS AND ALL
MOVE GENTLY ABOUT, SINGING OOMPAPA
POLITELY.

SMALL GENT (MUSIC STOPS): As a traveller of twenty-
seven years standing, I can fully appreciate the
advantages which will be conferred on us by the
railway this day opened. The manufacturers of the

Staffordshire Potteries have been getting further and further in the background for the last ten or twenty years, on account of the cost of carriage of their goods. Now that we can take advantage of the railway traffic I hope to see the day when we can successfully compete with the Northern Potteries...

WOOD: Hear hear!

SMALL GENT: ...and if the manufacturers do well, those about them, including the working classes, will partake of the same prosperity.

APPLAUSE. ALL MOVE AND OOMPAPA AGAIN.

Alderman Copeland...

ALDERMAN COPELAND DIRECTS HIS ATTENTION TO A NERVOUS WIFE.

COPELAND: I'll tell you another thing, how do you think I get my clay from Devon? By ship. Do you know how long it takes? Hm? Hm? Two months, or more. And when it gets here, its dry and mucky. A railway waggon full of clay is on its way from Plympton now. It will reach me in two days over the railway. Hm? Hm?

YOUNG WIFE: Wet and clean?

ALL TOAST: Wet and clean.

BANJO INSTRUMENTAL TO SONG BEGINS AGAIN.

ALL EXIT SINGING: The bold English navvies have laboured and made
A network of railways with pickaxe and spade.
None of us know where this progress will lead
But we can be certain we'll get there at speed.

FOUR GENTLEMEN ARE LEFT. THEY LIGHT CIGARS AND LISTEN. INSTRUMENTAL TO SONG CONTINUES.

CHRIS: Only see what railways have accomplished. Travelling has ceased to be an adventure of peril and great enterprise. Railways have now completely broken down the barriers which separated town from town and district from district. Travelling is no longer the luxury of the rich but the common enjoyment of all. Railways have made of England and Scotland, as it were, one large city with green fields,

hills and dales, rivers and lakes stretched out in
their midst. They have made travelling easy, rapid
and cheap. They have given a new power to the press
and to the post, serving to unite mind and matter and
to draw the ends of the earth together.

GENTLEMEN GO OUT. GILLIAN AND ANNE COME
TO CENTRE OF STAGE. BANJO MODULATES TO
MINOR KEY FOR NEXT SONG AND STOPS. LIGHTS
LOWER.


RAILWAY LINES

GILLIAN AND ANNE (UNNACOMPANIED): Railway lines;
    railway lines,
Roads of steel
Which join and part and bend
And then rush away
To meet again somewhere
Sometimes;
Like the lives of men.

Everywhere, look around,
In the air and underground
We're making progress
Yes, we are.
Machines making angry noises
Manned by men with unheard voices
Where's it leading?

People making things
Others breaking things,
Bigger words, louder fighting,
Where's it leading?
Moving forward, always proving something,
Writing books, pulling faces;
Catching trains and going places
Is it leading somewhere new?
Somewhere sunny?

Railway lines, railway lines,
Roads of steel
Which join and part and bend
And then rush away
To meet again somewhere,
Sometimes,

Like the lives of men.
LIGHTS FADE TO BLACKOUT.

# Part Two

THE STAGE CLOTH HAS BEEN CHANGED IN THE INTER-
VAL, AND NOW SHOWS THE FULL EXTENT OF THE
NORTH STAFFORDSHIRE TRACK IN 1900 FROM CREWE
IN THE NORTH TO COLWICH IN THE SOUTH, EAST
AND WEST TO DERBY AND MARKET DRAYTON. IT IS
NOW A COMPLEX OF LINES AND PLACE NAMES WITH
STOKE-ON-TRENT AT THE CENTRE.

RECORDED CHILDRENS' VOICES CHANTING: North
     Staffordshire Railway Loopy-la, I call Platform six,
     North Staffordshire Railway Loopy-la, I call Platform
     seven...etc (TO 'PLATFORM TEN').

     HOUSE LIGHTS FADE TO BLACKOUT DURING
     CHANT. SPOTLIGHT ON JEFF.


## INTRODUCTION SONG

JEFF SINGS (UNACCOMPANIED): We have now told half
     our story and the twentieth century's come,
     You've seen the rise of railways and the fortunes
     made by some –
     The planning and the digging and the laying of the line,
     The hopes and fears, the early years, the flavour of
     the line,

     You have seen the railway bosses and the profits that
     they made,
     Now see the power of unions and of the part they played,
     We'll take you through the Great World War, the rail-
     wayman in France,
     You will hear about the railway strikes and how they
     came to pass.

     You will see the well-known characters, the railway's
     household names,
     'W.D.' and Barnwell and the legends they became,
     Until Amalgamation with the L.M.S. at last,
     Made the great days of the Knotty just an echo in the
     past.

     SOUND OF PASSENGER TRAIN ARRIVING. ENTER
     W.D. PHILLIPS, FOLLOWED BY A REPORTER.
     BOTH ARE DRESSED AS IN 1900.

W.D. INTERVIEW

REPORTER: Mr W.D.Phillips, I presume?

W.D: That's right, lad.

REPORTER: Mr Phillips, as General Manager perhaps you'd be kind enough to answer a few questions for the Railway Magazine, concerning the North Staffordshire Railway - a subject, I need not add - of very considerable interest to my readers.

W.D.: I have been much surprised at the numbers who read your magazine and the intelligent interest taken in railway matters by the travelling public but I fear the North Staffordshire Railway is a very steady-going concern, which does not go in for anything sensational, likely to interest your readers.

REPORTER: Oh, I am sure there is plenty to interest them. Perhaps, as a commencement, Mr Phillips, you will locate the district that the North Staffordshire Railway serves.

W.D. (DEMONSTRATING ON FLOOR MAP): It is rather like an octopus, with its body at Stoke-on-Trent, stretching out its tentacles in every direction; northward to Macclesfield, where it joins the London and North Western, north west to Sandbach and Crewe, where again it joins the L.N.W.; westward to Market Drayton, where it joins the Great Western; southward to Norton Bridge and Colwich, where again it joins the L.N.W. and southeast to Burton and Derby, where it joins the Midland and Great Northern. Two hundred and four miles in all, the longest run, from Crewe to Derby, being only fifty-one. Have you got that?

REPORTER: Yes, thank you.

W.D.: Most of our runs are so short that the drivers are afraid to put on much speed, for fear of running twenty or thirty miles onto somebody else's line, before they can stop.

REPORTER: Thank you. That, at any rate, speaks well for the capabilities of the North Staffordshire loco-motives. Now, perhaps you can give us some details concerning your locomotive and rolling stock? Recently, I understand, the standard colour of the latter has been changed?

Stephenson scene

Pole dance

Pole dance

Oak Farm scene

Cutting of the first sod

1919 strike scene

Amalgamation scene

W.D.: Yes, we have recently altered the standard colour of our coaches. They are now painted a bright lake colour, and very smart they look, when first turned out, but the foul atmosphere of the Potteries is very hard on paint and varnish and soon dims their splendour.

REPORTER: May I ask you, Mr Phillips, about the traffic carried on the North Staffordshire Railway? It is, I think, largely mineral and merchandise?

W.D.: Not only minerals, though we transport millions of tons of coal, coke and earthenware, china, clay and flints. Beer from Burton amounting to over two hundred and twenty-five million gallons a year, also passes over our line.

REPORTER: You're not in the teetotal business then?

W.D.: Hardly.

REPORTER: Then, as to passenger traffic, do you specially cater for tourist or holiday traffic on the North Staffordshire Railway?

W.D.: As to passengers, we carry comparatively few, say seven and a half to eight million a year. The number of passenger trains in and out of Stoke Station is about two hundred and forty-five each day.

PASSENGER TRAIN SOUNDS, ENTER THE FIRST RAILWAYMAN, A PASSENGER GUARD IN KNOTTY UNIFORM, CARRYING HIS FLAGS. SALUTES.

FIRST RAILWAY MAN: Mr Phillips, you're wanted on Platform One. (GOES OFF)

W.D.: Thank you. Good day to you, young fellow. (GOES OFF)

REPORTER: Good day, sir. (GOES OFF.)

TRAIN SOUNDS LOUDER.


FIRST DAY SCENE

W.D. CROSSES STAGE, A RAILWAYMAN AND A YOUNG LAD COME ON. THE RAILWAYMAN TIPS HIS HAT. W.D. RESPONDS IN PASSING AND GOES OFF.

LAD: Who's that man with his head on one side?

RAILWAYMAN: Watch it, that's W.D.Phillips, General Manager. You want to keep out of his way, specially on your first day.

HE GOES OFF. GUITAR INSTRUMENTAL BEGINS. GILLIAN AND ANNE COME FORWARD, SINGING TOWARDS LOUDSPEAKER. LAD WATCHES.

## FIRST DAY ON THE LINE SONG

GILLIAN AND ANNE, ACCOMPANIED BY JEFF ON GUITAR: I'm just seventeen and I've left the clay,
I'm saved from coughing my life away,
I'm off to a world of wheels and smoke,
In the mighty engine sheds at Stoke.

ACCOMPANIMENT CONTINUES UNDER LOUD-SPEAKER VOICES.

LOUDSPEAKER VOICE (CHRIS BEECH): You started work at five-fifteen.

GIRLS SING: It's my first day out of the potbank,
It's my first day on the line.

LOUDSPEAKER VOICE (C.B.): There were twenty trains from five o'clock till about nine – there were twenty trains then.

TWO GIRLS (SING): My father helped me get the job,
It's start at the bottom and only six bob,
It's scrub and clean and polish and oil
But it's healthy work and worth the toil.

THE LAD HURRIES OFF.

LOUDSPEAKER VOICE (C.E. DAWSON): Of course, when you start at Stoke as a cleaner you start with rags and oil, you clean the engine wheels and tanks, the tenders, and everything had to be spick and span.

TWO GIRLS (SING): It's my first day out of the potbank,
It's my first day on the line.

LOUDSPEAKER VOICE (C.E.D.): After you've done about four years of cleaning, you are sent out on an engine as a fireman.

TWO GIRLS (SING): There's chance of promotion if I
    work hard,
  I'll have a train when I leave the yard,
  And proudly drive it along the track,
  With not much danger of getting the sack.

LOUDSPEAKER VOICE (C.E.D.): After a period of
  about twenty years you became a driver.

CHORUS: It's my first day out of the potbank,
  It's my first day on the line.

LOUDSPEAKER VOICE (C.E.D.): I myself started in nineteen nineteen and became a driver in nineteen forty-
  two.

TWO GIRLS (SING): I'm just seventeen and I've left the
    clay,
  I'm saved from coughing my life away,
  I'm off to a world of wheels and smoke
  In the mighty engine sheds at Stoke.

  It's my first day out of the potbank,
  It's my first day on the line.

  THE LAD RE-ENTERS, CROSSING THE STAGE.

LOUDSPEAKER VOICE (C.E.D.): Every boss at that
  particular time was very strict – discipline, discipline – it was all discipline.

  W.D. ENTERS, THE LAD SEES HIM AND HURRIEDLY
  TRIES TO AVOID MEETING HIM.


## W.D. COURTESY TALE

W.D: Boy, come here!

LAD: Yes sir.

W.D: Where were you going just then, boy? (PAUSE.)
  Wherever he may be, whatever he may be doing – a
  railwayman will always observe the courtesies to
  other railwaymen. Have you got that? Don't cross
  the road when you see me coming again.

LAD: Yes, Sir.

W.D: Right! Good day. (W.D. GOES OFF.)

  SOUND OF GOODS TRAIN MOVING THROUGH

STATION.

LOUDSPEAKER VOICE (FRANK OAKES): It's not unknown for a man to get sandwiched between two trains – in that case of course, the rule was that you must drop down flat, you drop down flat on your stomach.

THE LAD LISTENS TO THIS.


## PEELINGS TALE

AS BOY IS ABOUT TO GO, HE'S STOPPED BY A THIRD RAILWAYMAN.

THIRD RAILWAYMAN: When you get off this platform, lad, you need great presence of mind and strength of character. I will give you a illustration of this. I was in the office last week when the phone went and I picked it up. 'Hello', I said. 'Hello', said the voice at the other end, (it was Ross Holland). 'I've been knocked down in Harecastle Tunnel by the London Express'. So I thought, 'Here's a funny do, if he's been knocked down in Harecastle Tunnel by the London Express, how come he's talking to me at the other end of this phone then?'

LAD: How had it happened?

THIRD RAILWAYMAN: Ross Holland had been working in the tunnel when the signal came for the London Express, so he got to the side, pressed tight to the side, with his stomach in and chin in, London Express came charging through, fifty miles an hour, eighteen inches away, when a waiter inside thought, 'Well, I'm in a tunnel, out the way, I'll chuck me potato pillings out the window.' So he did and Mr Holland, was caught by them on the back of the head and thrown off balance. Now this is where his great presence of mind and strength of character came in, instead of falling across the rail, which would have meant, whisssh, cut in three or four bits and very nasty, he fell along the rail and lay there, with great presence of mind and strength of character, mark you, while the train went past.


HIGH WHISTLE OF APPROACHING EXPRESS STARTS.

They got the waiter at Euston – suspended him.

GOES OFF. EXPRESS WHISTLES AND ROARS
THROUGH.

## SIGNAL BELL TEST

BEFORE THE LAD CAN ESCAPE, ENTER A FOURTH
RAILWAYMAN (SIGNAL INSPECTOR).

INSPECTOR: So, you've been learning the bell
code, have you?

THE LAD NODS.

Is line clear for branch passenger train?

LAD (ALWAYS WITH GESTURES): Ding (PAUSE) ding
ding ding.

INSPECTOR: Is line clear for plate layer's lorry re-
quiring to pass through tunnel?

LAD: Ding ding (PAUSE.) ding (PAUSE.) ding ding.

INSPECTOR: Is line clear for fish, meat, fruit, horse,
cattle or perishable train, composed of coaching
stock?

LAD: Ding ding ding ding.

INSPECTOR: Ding!

LAD: Ding.

INSPECTOR: I'll see about you, lad.

HE GOES OFF. LIGHTS CHANGE TO NIGHT, LAD
TURNS COLLAR UP AND PACES ABOUT, WAITING
IN RAIN. GUITAR PLAYS QUIETLY INSTRUMENTAL
FOR MOON SONG. RHYTHMIC KNOCKING ON ROS-
TRUM.

## KNOCKING UP

LOUDSPEAKER VOICE (HARRY SHARRATT): If you were
cleaning on the night shift at about three a.m. they
would give you written instructions to go and knock up
four or five drivers and firemen, all at different
times. Often, there would be about half an hour be-

tween calls and, in the event of rain, we should have
to take shelter in someone's doorway. In the event
of the driver not answering to the knock, you would
have to repeat it louder and possibly shout.

LAD (SHOUTS): Wake up, driver! Time you were up!
Can't you hear me?

A DRIVER ENTERS WITH TEA CAN AND CROSSES
THE STAGE.

DRIVER: All right, I've got neighbours, you know.
Don't have to wake up the whole street.

HE GOES OFF. QUIET MOURNFUL SOUND OF
WHISTLE AT NIGHT FOLLOWED BY DISTANT
SHUNTING SOUNDS. GUITAR STARTS INSTRUMEN-
TAL FOR MOON SONG. THE LAD RE-ENTERS
WITH PLATFORM BARROW. FIRST AND THIRD
RAILWAYMEN ENTER WITH MAILBAGS AND NOTE
PADS. THEY SORT THEM OUT AS THEY SING.


THE MOON SONG

AT THE END OF THE SONG THE THIRD RAILWAYMAN
GOES OFF WITH EMPTY BARROW. THE FIRST RAIL-
WAY MAN STAGGERS OFF, CARRYING ALL MAIL-
BAGS.

BOTH SING: The moon has raised her lamp above,
    To light the way to thee, my love,
    To light the way to thee, my love.
    Her rays upon the waters play,
    To tell me eyes more bright than they
    Are watching through the night,
    Are watching through the night.
    I come, I come, my heart's delight,
    I come, I come, I come, my heart's delight,
    I come, I come, I come, my heart's delight.

    The moon has raised  her lamp above,
    To light the way to thee, my love
    To light the way to thee, my love.

THEY GO OFF. LIGHTS FADE TO VERY DARK FOR
SCENE OF SHUNTING AT NIGHT. PENETRATING
STEAM HISS FADES IN AND CONTINUES FOR
WHOLE SEQUENCE.

SHUNTING SEQUENCE: 1, FIRST UNION MEETINGS

SHUNTER ENTERS, CROSSES STAGE AND GOES OFF.

LOUDSPEAKER ANNOUNCEMENT: Sunday, February
the fourteenth, nineteen hundred and four. First
meeting of the Footplate Union at Stoke.

THE FIRST RAILWAYMAN, AS UNION SECRETARY
ENTERS LIT BY A SINGLE SPOTLIGHT IN ONE
CORNER.

UNION SECRETARY: Brothers, I'll read the minutes.
At a meeting of the Enginemen, Firemen and Cleaners,
Mr Parfitt, the organising Secretary of the above,
explained the objects and benefits of the Amalgamated
Society of Locomotive Enginemen and Firemen and
succeeded in opening a branch at Stoke, eighteen
paying entrance fees. After a very interesting address,
it was decided to hold another meeting on February
the twenty-eighth, for the selection of officers. Mr
W. Thomson occupied the chair.

Can I ask for a member to propose that these minutes
be accepted as a true record?

THE SPOTLIGHT ON THE UNION SECRETARY GOES
OUT. STEAM HISS BLASTS IN VERY LOUD. ENTER
THE SECOND RAILWAYMAN AS A DRIVER, THE
THIRD AS A FIREMAN, THE LAD AS A SHUNTER.
(HE'S A BIG LAD). THEY YELL TO ONE ANOTHER
OVER THE DIN.

FIREMAN (TO DRIVER): What did you join for?

DRIVER: To get me rights.

SHUNTER: Have you joined the new Union?

DRIVER: Course I bloody have.

SHUNTER ( BLOWS WHISTLE SIGNAL, THEN SHOUTS
TO DRIVER): Bushbury Sidings!

THE STAGE IS VERY DARK. THE SHUNTER STANDS
IN A TIGHT SHAFT OF LIGHT BY THE WIDE CEN-
TRAL ENTRANCE, HOLDING HIS SHUNTING POLE
IN ONE HAND AND SIGNAL LANTERN IN THE OTHER.
AFTER EACH WHISTLE SIGNAL (TO THE UNSEEN
SIGNALMAN IN HIS BOX) HE TURNS TO FACE UP
THE ENTRANCE AND SHOUTS TO THE DRIVER THE

NAME OF THE SECTION THEY ARE SHUNTING
ONTO. THEN HE BRINGS THE ENGINE ON BY
SHOWING A GREEN LIGHT. THE HISS IS RE-
PLACED BY THE SOUND OF THE ENGINE SLOWLY
APPROACHING. DRIVER AND FIREMAN ULTIMATELY
APPEAR NEAR HIM AT EITHER SIDE OF THE EN-
TRANCE, ONLY THEIR FACES LIT AS THOUGH
PEERING OUT OF EITHER SIDE OF THE CAB. THE
SHUNTER FLICKS HIS LAMP TO RED TO STOP THE
ENGINE. THERE IS A CLANK AS THE WAGONS ARE
UNHOOKED, THE SHUNTER LEVERING HIS POLE
INTO THE DARKNESS. THEN HE HURRIES ACROSS
THE STAGE FOLLOWING THE SOUND OF THE
RUMBLING WAGONS TILL THEY HIT THE OTHERS
ALREADY ON THAT TRACK WITH A CRASH. THE
UNION SECRETARY'S SPOTLIGHT COMES ON, THE
LIGHT STEAM HISS TAKES OVER, THE SHUNTER
SENDS THE ENGINE SLOWLY BACK FOR ANOTHER
SHUNT BY FLICKING HIS LIGHT TO WHITE, MOVING
INTO HIS FIRST POSITION DURING EACH OF THE
UNION SECRETARY'S SPEECHES. THIS SEQUENCE
OCCURS THREE TIMES.

AT THE END OF THE FIRST ONE:

UNION SECRETARY: March the twenty-sixth, nineteen
hundred and five. It was proposed by Mr Foster,
seconded by Mr J. Dunn and carried unanimously that
the Branch Secretary be instructed to write to Mr
Adams, Loco Superintendent, to express the feelings
of the Branch, regarding harsh suspensions and
punishments the locomotivemen are subject to and
ask him to tender mercy with justice.

SHUNTER (WHISTLE SIGNAL THEN SHOUTS TO
DRIVER): Back Row!


## SHUNTING SEQUENCE: SECOND PHASE AS BEFORE

UNION SECRETARY: February the twenty third, nineteen
hundred and eight. Considerable discussion took
place, respecting the severe suspensions and the
following resolution was carried unanimously: 'Any
member who meets with a mishap, or is in any difficulty, must report at once to the Branch Secretary,
who shall place particulars before a deputation, which

shall be appointed to interview the Superintendent in the matter, so that the deputation may be present before the member is suspended.'

SHUNTER (WHISTLE SIGNAL): Number nine!

## SHUNTING SEQUENCE: THIRD PHASE AS BEFORE

AS THE SHUNTER REACHES THE OTHER SIDE OF STAGE W.D.PHILLIPS ENTERS UNSEEN BY HIM.

SHUNTER (SHOUTS): Come on, bang the bastards up!

W.D: Shunter! Those waggons may have no father, but I am their rich uncle.

HE GOES OFF MAKING A SALUTE TO FIREMAN AND DRIVER. THE SHUNTER SENDS THE ENGINE BACK. THE UNION SECRETARY'S LIGHT COMES ON.

UNION SECRETARY: July the eighteenth, nineteen hundred and nine. The Branch Secretary moved the following resolution: 'That a debating class be formed in connection with the Branch, the main object to be the advancement and education of the members in social, political and trade union matters and to render them more efficient in the art of extempore speaking.'

HE GOES OFF.

## SHUNTING SEQUENCE: 2. BOTHY SCENE

SHUNTER (SHOUTS): Right, that's the lot, lads. Tea up.

HISS STOPS. DRIVER AND FIREMAN COME ON WITH TEA CAN.

FIREMAN: Ah, I left school when I was fourteen and there's nowt wrong with me.

DRIVER: You think so?

THEY CROUCH IN A CORNER POURING THE TEA.

SHUNTER: Well, what was it this time?

DRIVER: You what?

SHUNTER: You and your Union whatsit classes.

DRIVER: We had a debate on individualism and socialism and the capitalist exploitation of the introduction of modern machinery.

FIREMAN: Hip, hip, hooray.

SHUNTER: Ah mate, what you want these debating classes for? You can read and write, you know your job. What more do you want? Leave the big words to the big nobs.

ENTER UNION SECRETARY

FIREMAN: Here comes Union Jack.

UNION SECRETARY: Brothers, I have come with special information, which I have been requested to circulate. The Directors have granted us special concessions. (CROUCHES DOWN WITH THEM) Here they are: One: All drivers and firemen commencing a period of duty on train work to be paid full train rate up to ten hours, — six hours forty minutes on Sundays. Two: If, after two years on the four and threepenny rate, firemen can pass the usual driving examination they will be paid at the four and sixpenny rate. That's all thanks.

HE GOES OFF.

FIREMAN: That's all right, ain't it!

SHUNTER: Who the bloody hell does he think he is? Talks like one of the bosses.

DRIVER: He's doing it for you too.

SHUNTER: I don't want him doing anything for me. The Company is doing a fine job running the railway, mate...You and your classes...Next thing you know, the unions'll be wanting to take everything over.

DRIVER: And a bloody good job they'd do. Think I like emptying ashpits just to make up time, after I've come off the footplate? From driver to ashpit cleaner all in one day.

SHUNTER: And another thing, he's going to get us into trouble if he don't stop coming around here. They don't like it.

DRIVER: I couldn't care less. You're just governed by fear. Well, not this lad, see.

THEY GO OFF. THE DRIVER LEAVES HIS HAT ON
THE GROUND AND RETRIEVES IT DURING THE
CHAIRMAN'S SPEECH.

(LIGHTS ILLUMINATE LONG SIGNBOARDS HIGH IN
THE AUDITORIUM SAYING 'STAFFORDSHIRE
ADVERTISER' AND 'EVENING SENTINEL')

LOUDSPEAKER ANNOUNCEMENT: Newsflash! Railwaymen's strike! Four thousand on strike in Liverpool.
A Liverpool correspondent, telegraphing on Tuesday
night, stated: 'The railwaymen's strike showed signs
of extending in Liverpool today. The number of strikers
has increased to about four thousand.'

SIGNBOARD LIGHTS OUT. CORNER SECTION OF THE
STAGE IS LIT.

SHUNTING SEQUENCE: 3. CHAIRMAN'S REPORT

CHAIRMAN ENTERS WITH W.D. THEY BRING ON TWO
CHAIRS. CHAIRMAN HAS GLASS OF BRANDY.

CHAIRMAN: Well, gentlemen, shall we get down to business?
(SITS) I'm afraid that our promises of last February
were rather too optimistic. This will be the main point
of my speech to the shareholders tomorrow. I'm sure
that they will agree that circumstances beyond our
control did somewhat upset our calculations in respect of the five per cent dividend, which we promised
them at the last meeting. Labour troubles all over the
country, especially the London dock strikes and the
more recent chaos in Liverpool, will only allow us to
pay out four and a half per cent this year. I'm sure
you all agree. However, I will be so bold as to
promise them a full five per cent next year, providing of course that the abominable industrial conditions beyond the Potteries resume their normal
character. I shall then proceed with the Expenditure,
which is largely due to our policy of lengthening the
platforms at Etruria, Longport and so on, the new
engines and then the passenger receipts, (I say, Mr
Phillips weren't the takings on Coronation Day dis-
appointing?), and then I shall venture to propose the
abolition of second class carriages on our Railway.
Yes...yes...I thought you'd object to that but you

must realise, gentlemen, that our figures for the
half-year just ended show that the popularity of the
third class coaches is on the increase, while that of
the first and second class is decidedly decreasing.
And of course we would never dream of abolishing
the first class and, on the other thand, the third
class coaches are made so very comfortable. I'm
sure you agree with me. Finally, I shall give the
usual thanks to the General Manager and all his able
staff for the continuing loyalty they have always
shown to our interests. Gentlemen, I propose a toast
to larger dividends in the coming year. Cheers.

THEY GO OFF. STAGE BRIGHTENS. BIRDS SING.
TWO RAILWAYMEN IN SHIRT SLEEVES AND WAIST-
COATS STROLL ON WITH SHOVELS, AS PLATE-
LAYERS.

## SHUNTING SEQUENCE: 4. W.D.'S RABBIT

FIRST PLATELAYER (TO AUDIENCE): Here, I wanna
tell you something. Y'see, two platelayers were
walking, along the track, y'see, having a fag, y'see,
slacking y'see, when the driver of a passing train,
he waved...

SECOND PLATELAYER: Y'see.

FIRST PLATELAYER: Who's telling this story? Well,
stop enlarging your part. He waved, y'see, to warn
'em that W.D. Phillips was coming along the track...
(SOUND OF TRAIN PASSING)...that was the train
y'see. But they didn't catch his meaning, y'see...
they thought he'd seen a rabbit.

BIRDS AGAIN.

SECOND PLATELAYER: Where?

FIRST PLATELAYER: Over there. Come on.

SECOND PLATELAYER: Aye.

THEY GO OVER AND PREPARE TO DIG. ENTER
W.D. PHILLIPS. THE PLATELAYER HASTILY
HIDES HIS CIGARETTE.

W.D: Platelayers, why aren't you working?...Eh, lad,
do you realise you're on fire?

FIRST PLATELAYER: Y'see, Mr Phillips, y'see the

driver of that train, y'see 'e waved and 'e pointed and we thought 'd'd seen a rabbit.

PAUSE.

W.D: I'm the bloody rabbit! (HE GOES OFF.)

FIRST PLATELAYER: Heh, when that old bugger dies, his ghost'll walk the Knotty.

W.D. (FROM OFF): Platelayer, if I do, I'll take you with me!

THE TWO PLATELAYERS GO OFF. LIGHTS DIM A LITTLE. GUITAR INSTRUMENTAL TO MOON SONG BEGINS

SHUNTING SEQUENCE: 5. GOLDEN SOVEREIGNS

AS THE LOUDSPEAKER VOICE COMES IN, A LADY AND GENTLEMAN CROSS THE STAGE PRECEDED BY A PORTER WITH LUGGAGE. THE LADY AND GENTLEMAN EMBRACE AND PART, THE GENTLEMAN GIVES THE PORTER A SOVEREIGN THEN WAVES AS THE PORTER AND LADY GO OFF. THE GENTLEMAN GOES. PORTER RE-ENTERS.

LOUDSPEAKER VOICE (FRED ADAMS): The people that was good to us in the Potteries was Bamfords of Uttoxeter, they was a golden sovereign; Royce, Mrs Royce, Rolls-Royce of Derby, they was a golden sovereign; Francis Joseph, Joseph of Alsager, Settles, he was a golden sovereign; and Lady Torrington, the race-horse owner, if you got her, that was a golden sovereign. The valet of the Duke of Westminster, from Chester, if you got him, that was a golden sovereign. But there was lots more and, if you got a golden sovereign, it was a lot in them days, you know.

THE PORTER GAZES LOVINGLY AT THE SOVER-EIGN. ENTER W.D. PHILLIPS.

W.D: Porter, what are you messing about at? You've a big head but there's not much in it.

PORTER: Aye, but at least it's set on straight.

BOTH GO OFF. W.D. DISCOMFITED. SIGNBOARD LIGHTS ON. BANJO INSTRUMENTAL BEGINS.

LOUDSPEAKER ANNOUNCEMENT: News Flash! Railway strike spreading. Armed Convoys in Liverpool.

TWO GIRLS IN SHAWLS WITH SHOPPING BASKETS COME ON.

## 1911 STRIKE SONG

GIRLS SING (WITH BANJO ACCOMPANIMENT):
Good day, you there duckie,
Good day, you there gal.
Where is your old man today,
At home or on the rail?

He's out being a picketer,
His union code is strong,
He's striking for his principle
For righting workers' wrongs.

My man he went to work today,
He wants no kind of trouble,
The owners treat him very well,
His fellow men they grumble.

We don't know what it's all about,
We don't know what they're doing,
They only tell us that they think
They're gaining more than losing.

Ours is only one concern
That's bread and meat for all
Clothes for kids and coal for warmth
And come when menfolk call.

BANJO ACCOMPANIMENT CONTINUES. THE GIRLS MOVE TO SIDE OF THE STAGE AND STAY THERE. SIGNBOARD LIGHTS ON.

## 1911 STRIKE SEQUENCE: 1. UNION SECRETARY

LOUDSPEAKER VOICE: About two hundred men at St Mary's Goods Yard, Derby, struck at eight o'clock today.

General cessation of work on all railway lines at Leeds, eight o'clock today.

The men of the Great Central and Great Northern
system at Leicester struck at nine o'clock this
morning.

SIGNBOARD LIGHTS OFF. THE UNION SECRETARY'S
SPOTLIGHT COMES ON. ENTER UNION SECRETARY
IN HIS CORNER. BANJO STOPS.

## STRIKE SEQUENCE: 2. CHAIRMAN ON PHONE AND CHALKING SCENE

AS THE CHAIRMAN SPEAKS THE FIREMAN CHALKS
TWICE RIGHT ACROSS THE STAGE ON EITHER SIDE
OF HIM 'WE WANT RECOGNITION'

CHAIRMAN: Yes, speaking.... That's a gross exagger-
ation, young man. I can tell you with complete authority
that, as far as the North Staffordshire Railway is
concerned, there are no labour difficulties. Of course,
as the London and Northwestern trains have been
affected by the strike, passengers on long distance
journeys will have to put up with some delays. I can
assure you that the local trains are running to schedule
...Of course, it is impossible to predict any further
developments but I will try to keep you informed if
anything does come up.

HE GOES OFF. BY THIS TIME FIREMAN HAS
CHALKED ON THE FLOOR: 'WE WANT RECOGNITION.
WE WANT RECO-' WHEN W.D. ENTERS AND STOPS
HIM, PUTTING HIS STICK IN MIDDLE OF THE 'O'.
FIREMAN COMPLETES 'O'.

FIREMAN (STANDS): There's no harm in chalking on the
pavement is there?

W.D: No harm at all, Fireman, but you won't get a pension that way.

HE GOES OFF. BANJO STARTS AGAIN. FIREMAN
COMPLETES WRITING. DRIVER ENTERS AND LOOKS
AT IT CRITICALLY.

TWO GIRLS (SING): We don't know what it's all about,
We don't know what they're doing,
They only tell us that they think
They're gaining more than losing.

Ours is only one conern
That's bread and meat for all,
Clothes for kids and coal for warmth
And come when menfolks call.

BANJO CONTINUES. SIGNBOARD LIGHTS ON.

LOUDSPEAKER VOICE: News Flash! The signal to
cease work was received by the Secretary of the
Stoke Branch of the ASRS at seven-fifteen on Thursday
night and steps were at once taken with the object of
bringing out those railwaymen who happened to be
trade unionists. A great deal of success attended
these efforts.

THE SHUNTER COMES ON, WITH POLE, AT OTHER
SIDE OF STAGE.

## 1911 STRIKE SEQUENCE: 3. PICKET SCENE

THE UNION SECRETARY ENTERS WITH A TELEGRAM
AND GOES TO THE DRIVER AND FIREMAN. BANJO
STOPS.

UNION SECRETARY: Brothers, here it is. The telegram
from the Head Office of the four big unions. I will
read it to you: 'Your liberty at stake. All railwaymen
must strike at once. Loyalty to each other means
victory. Signed Williams, Fox, Lowthe, Chorlton.'
Brothers, we're on strike.

DRIVER: What do we have to do?

UNION SECRETARY: Well, every man working on the
railway must be fetched out, but it's got to be done
peacefully. Look, brothers, never in the history of
this country have the workers had such a chance to
strengthen their position and it all rests with us.

SHUNTER: I don't know what you're on about. I've got
no practical grievances and every time I've had one
I've always been received courteously.

UNION SECRETARY: That's fine but every time you've
gone up to them they could have sacked you, victi-
mixed you. You've got to have a Union behind you so
they can't do that. And we've got to get rid of the
Conciliation Boards. Grievances take months, years

to go through and when there's an award it's not official — the Company can interpret it which way they like, mutilate it even.

SHUNTER: But if I go out, I'm going to be victimized all the same. What if I do throw in my lot with you, what then? Are you going to protect me? You're all in when you want something and out when you don't...

UNION SECRETARY: Look, the official telegram refers to all railwaymen, so I can promise that we'll carry you through. The Union will protect your job, see, if you throw in your lot with us.

SHUNTER: I'll have to think about it. I've got a job to keep.

BANJO INSTRUMENTAL BASED ON PREVIOUS SONG BEGINS. SIGNBOARD LIGHTS ON.

LOUDSPEAKER ANNOUNCEMENT: News Flash! August the eighteenth. Pickets were posted at various points and our informant stated that since ten o'clock last night not more than half a dozen drivers had gone in. It is difficult to ascertain what proportion of employees of the North Staffordshire Railway are members of the trade unions. The locomen — enginemen, firemen and cleaners — are best organised and a large majority of these have come out. In various parts of Stoke today may be seen groups of railwaymen, in many cases on picket duty, discussing the situation.

OVER THE SOUND OF THE BANJO INSTRUMENTAL A SILENT BATTLE WITH THE BLACKLEG SHUNTER IS PLAYED OUT: THE UNION SECRETARY HANDS OUT THREE PLACARDS ON SHORT POLES (PLACARDS READ 'STOKE STRIKES FOR UNION RECOGNITION', ALSAGER STRIKES FOR UNION RECOGNITION', 'MACCLESFIELD STRIKES FOR UNION RECOGNITION'). THE DRIVER AND FIREMAN EACH TAKE ONE — SHUNTER REFUSES — UNION SECRETARY TAKES THIRD AND THEY FORM A PICKET LINE — CHAIRMAN APPEARS — DRIVER AND FIREMAN TURN AWAY — UNION SECRETARY MAKES A FIRM STAND — DRIVER AND FIREMAN RETURN — SHUNTER APPROACHES LINE — THEY CLOSE UP — SHUNTER TRIES TO BREAK THROUGH WITH HIS POLE — THEY CLOSE RIGHT UP — SHUNTER TURNS

AWAY – DRIVER BREAKS FROM PICKET LINE AND
PUTS HIS HAND ON THE SHUNTER'S SHOULDER.
BANJO STOPS.

DRIVER: Homeward bound.

SHUNTER TURNS TO LEAVE AND IS STOPPED
BY CHAIRMAN.

CHAIRMAN: My man, you are not alone. Quite a number
of the Company's employees still remain loyal and
are perfectly willing to work, just as you are. I
tell you what, as far as you are concerned, the
Company will pay you time and a half.

UNION SECRETARY: That's grossly unfair. The law
allows a company to give a bonus of fifty per cent to
men who remain working, whereas if we offer a
bribe to men not to work we will be prosecuted. In
Crewe blacklegs are being sheltered in the London
and North Western Hotel and are living there in first
rate style and have got everything they require. Is
that fair?

CHAIRMAN: Fair or unfair, we are making an urgent
representation to the Mayor of Stoke-on-Trent for
police protection and, if you do want to work, we'll
see that you don't suffer any reprisals. (TO SHUN-
TER.) What do you say?

SHUNTER: I darena go.

UNION SECRETARY: Good man. (TO CHAIRMAN.)
And the drivers from Derby and Liverpool that you've
wired for, they're going to be stopped too. And it's
no use calling in the police, because it's all going
to be done very peacefully.

CHAIRMAN: This is preposterous. Up to six o'clock
last evening I had no idea that there was trouble of
any kind brewing among our employees. None of you
had made any complaints as to wages, hours of duty or
anything else.

UNION SECRETARY: Sir, it is very peculiar that you
should be the only employer throughout the kingdom
who did not see what was coming. It has been a
well-known fact in the railway world for years.

CHAIRMAN: What are your grievances, then? Many of you

have been in the employ of the Company from twenty to
forty years and you are all proud of the Company,
I'm sure. The North Stafford can boast of a clean
record, so far as accidents causing loss of life are
concerned  This is due in no small measure to the
faithfulness of the company's employees.

UNION SECRETARY: I know that many of us in the North
Stafford have no personal grievance at all but, speaking generally, we're in sympathy with the men of
other companies who have great and serious ones.

CHAIRMAN: So, you have gone on strike without the
slightest excuse and without any kind of provocation.

DRIVER: Can I say something?

CHAIRMAN: Yes, of course.

DRIVER: I read the report of the last shareholders'
meeting. This was in the Sentinel sometime last week.
Any road, the report says this was the most pros-
perous half year they've had. We...er congratulate
the company on its prosperity but we would like that
the Company would give us badly paid men more pay
for our work. I think it's us men who bring the bulk
of the profits. It's us that do the bloody work.

CHAIRMAN (DIRECT TO UNION SECRETARY): I see
it's a fight to the finish. Let me warn you that, since
you went on strike in such an exceedingly unprovoked
way, and have taken such a supreme action without
the slightest motive, the sympathies of the public will
be with the companies.

UNION SECRETARY: You've made yourself very clear,
sir. And our reply is: 'Ditto'.

W.D. ENTERS WITH A TELEGRAM AND HANDS IT
TO THE CHAIRMAN. THE FIREMAN GOES OFF TO
COLLECT ANOTHER DURING THE CHAIRMAN'S
SPEECH.

CHAIRMAN: Gentlemen, I am happy to say that the strike
is over. Here are the terms of the settlement (READS
TELEGRAM.) 'Signed on August the eighteenth,
nineteen eleven, at the Board of Trade, on behalf of
the Railway Companies and of the Joint Executives of
the Trade Unions of Railway Employees and of the
Government and the Board of Trade:

Section One: Strike to be terminated forthwith. All men to return to work at once.

Section Two: All the men involved in the present dispute, who present themselves for work within reasonable time, to be reinstated by the Companies and no one to be subjected to proceedings for breach of contract, or otherwise penalised.

Section Three: The Conciliation Boards to be convened for the purposes of settling forthwith the questions at present in dispute.

Section Four: Both parties to give every assistance to the Special Commission of Enquiry, the immediate appointment of which the Government has announced. '

THE UNION SECRETARY HAS GOT HIS COPY FROM THE FIREMAN AND NODS TO RAILWAYMEN IN CONFIRMATION.

And this, gentlemen, is signed by representatives of the Companies and of the Trade Unions. I congratulate you.

BANJO ACCOMPANIMENT TO SONG BEGINS AND CARRIES ON THROUGHOUT. ALL GO OFF EXCEPT DRIVER AND FIREMAN. A RAILWAYMAN BRINGS ON A TEA CAN AND A BARROW. THEY SHARE TEA DURING SONG.

## DRIVER AND FIREMAN SONG

DRIVER: It's a good job has the driver, it's the best one on the line,
He makes no end of money - when he works no end of time.
He goes on when they want him and he comes off when he can,
Yes, there's no mistake, the driver is a very lucky man.

FIREMAN: It's not all beer and skittles, this bloomin' job of mine,
And it's not a bed of roses, isn't firing on the line,
You don't get too much money, you get lots of slack instead
And they teach you how to work at night to earn your daily bread.

DRIVER: Quite a nice job has the driver, working in the
oil and grease,
Some day his engine they may clean, for wonders
never cease,
But until he sees that lucky day, as every driver
knows,
He'll spend many a happy hour scraping grease from
off his clothes.

FIREMAN: I often wonder if I'll ever get a driver's job,
For I'm sick and tired of firing six hours for thirty
bob,
Perhaps I'll fire until I die and then to Heaven I'll
go,
Or perhaps I will be firing for the old Lad down
below.

DRIVER: And what about the driver when his working
days are o'er?
They let him toil and sweat and boil till he can do
no more,
Will he get a handsome pension when the tree has lost
its sap?
No! Just like the engine that he works, he's placed
among the scrap.

BOTH: It's a shame they work the drivers till of age
they nearly drop,

Why can't they have a pension, like a postman or
a 'slop'?
They earn it, they deserve it and contented they would
be –

FIREMAN: Besides, 'twould mean promotion and there'd
be a chance for me!

THE SOUND OF A DISTANT SHELL BARRAGE BE-
GINS AND CONTINUES, FADING DURING HARRY
SHARRATT'S PASSAGE.


GREAT WAR SEQUENCE

SEVERAL OF THE RAILWAYMEN NOW COME ON IN
KHAKI JACKETS AND MILITARY HATS BRINGING A
STRETCHER, RIFLE, BLANKETS, BELTS, UNIFORMS
FOR THE DRIVER AND FIREMAN. DURING THE LOUD–

SPEAKER VOICES ALL CHANGE AND PREPARE FOR
THE SEQUENCE. THIS IS ALL PLAYED IN A SLIGHTLY
SMALLER AREA THAN THE FULL ACTING AREA, ALL
THE CAST SITTING OR CROUCHING AT THE SIDE
WHEN NOT IN A SCENE. SAPPER SHARRATT IS PLAYED
BY THE FIREMAN, HIS DRIVER BY THE DRIVER. THE
PLATFORM BARROW IS USED AS THE FOOTPLATE
OF THE TROOP TRAIN.

LOUDSPEAKER VOICE (TOM UNDERWOOD): You see,
    war breaks out in nineteen fourteen.

(KEN JACKSON): I joined the Fifth North Staffords. I did
    six months in them. Then I weighed things up and I
    thought to meself like, I'm not going to march on my
    bloody way to bits (LAUGHS.) carrying ninety-eight
    pounds on me back – I got a transfer to the Royal
    Engineers.

(TOM UNDERWOOD): I said, 'What. Make me go? They
    couldn't, 'I said 'because I'd stand agin a wall
    and be shot first,' I says, 'and I'm no use to 'em
    dead.' (LAUGHS) Was that courage?

(HARRY SHARRATT): I went out to France in nineteen-
    fifteen and I was there for a considerable time. At
    the end of September, I got hit by a piece of shell. I
    cane out of hospital, went to England, came out to
    France again on the first draft to Rouen, where I
    worked on the docks.


GREAT WAR SEQUENCE: SCENE ONE

SAPPER SHARRATT AND ANOTHER SOLDIER CAR-
RYING A HEAVY BOX.

SOLDIER: How are you then, mate?

SHARRATT: All right, thanks.

SOLDIER: Been up the trenches, then?

SHARRATT: Aye, I came out to France in February of
    nineteen-fifteen and I was there till September.

    SERGEANT MAJOR ENTERS.

SGT. MAJOR (BLOWS WHISTLE): Break for five minutes!

    THE SIT ON THE BOX CENTRE STAGE.

SHARRATT: Then I got hit by a piece of shell, which smashed me rifle on me back and put me in hospital till after Christmas.

SGT. MAJOR (BLOWS WHISTLE): Break for five minutes!

SOLDIER: You're a railwayman, aren't you?

SHARRATT: Yes, I am, aye.

SOLDIER: You ought to jon the R.O.D.s mate.

SHARRATT: R.O.D.s, what are they?

SOLDIER: Oh, the Railway Operating Division.

SHARRATT: Well, how do you get into that?

SOLDIER: Easy, all you do is write a special letter of application, you know, giving all your railway experience and hope for the best.

SGT. MAJOR (BLOWING WHISTLE): Back to work!

SAPPER WRITES

LOUDSPEAKER VOICE (HARRY SHARRATT): So I immediately wrote back and told him I'd been a fireman on the North Staffordshire Railway. The next thing that happened – it was about a week elapsed and I was still waiting.


GREAT WAR SEQUENCE: SCENE TWO

ALL SOLDIERS LINE UP IN FRONT OF SGT. MAJOR.

SGT. MAJOR: On parade!

Parade, attention! Right dress! Sapper Sharratt!

SHARRATT (STEPS FORWARD): Sergeant Major!

SGT. MAJOR: You're for draft today.

SHARRATT: Sergeant Major!

PRIVATE: That's what you get for applying for a job on the railway.

SGT. MAJOR: Parade, to your work...Dismiss!

THEY DISMISS EXCEPT SAPPER SHARRATT.

LOUDSPEAKER VOICE (HARRY SHARRATT): Well, it's

rather unusual to call me a draft on my own. There were two thousand men there.

LIGHTS CHANGE TO NIGHT.

## GREAT WAR SEQUENCE: SCENE THREE

THE NOTES OF A TRUMPET CALL – 'LIGHTS OUT' – PICKED OUT ON MANDOLINE. SHARRATT UNROLLS BLANKET AND LIES DOWN. TWO OTHER SOLDIERS DO THE SAME.

LOUDSPEAKER VOICE (HARRY SHARRATT): Oh, I'm going back to the trenches again.

LIGHTS CHANGE FOR DAY SOUND OF TRUMPET REVEILLE – ALL JUMP UP – DRUM BEAT STARTS (PLAYED ON FRONT OF BANJO) CORPORAL COMES TO SHARRATT.

## GREAT WAR SEQUENCE: SCENE FOUR

CORPORAL: You Sapper Sharratt?

SHARRATT: Yes, Corporal.

CORPORAL: You're going back to your regiment.

SHARRATT: Yes, Corporal.

CORPORAL: You'll come with me to the armoury, where you'll get a hundred rounds of amunition, a rifle and your equipment.

SHARRATT: Thank you, Corporal.

CORPORAL: Think nothing of it, Sapper. Left...left... left.

THEY MARCH TO WHERE A RIFLE LIES ON STAGE – SHARRATT PICKS IT UP. THE CORPORAL GOES. OFFICER CROSSES – SHARRATT STOPS AND SLAPS RIFLE BUTT IN SALUTE.

## GREAT WAR SEQUENCE: SCENE FIVE

CAPTAIN: Hallo, Sapper, what's your name?

SHARRATT: Sapper Sharratt, sir.

CAPTAIN: Oh, you're Sapper Sharratt, are you? I remember signing your papers. I hope that the next time you come here you'll enjoy yourself and we promise to try and make you as comfortable as we can.

SHARRATT: Thank you, sir.

OFFICER GOES. SHARRATT GIVES V-SIGN TO HIS RETREATING BACK.

LOUDSPEAKER VOICE (HARRY SHARRATT): I was thinking something else at the same time.

SHARRATT MARCHES TO SERGEANT MAJOR. DRUM BEAT STOPS.


GREAT WAR SEQUENCE: SCENE SIX

SGT. MAJOR: Sapper Sharratt!

SHARRATT: Sergeant Major!

SGT. MAJOR: Today, you're going to the Railway Operating Division R.E., for a test.

SHARRATT SETS HIS RIFLE BUTT SLOWLY DOWN ON THE FLOOR.

LOUDSPEAKER VOICE (HARRY SHARRATT): After that, I heard nothting else, my head soaring up in the air.

SGT. MAJOR: Now, you'll give this to the R.T.O. at Rouen Station, this is your travel pass, you'll need this if you get stranded and need extra rations and you'll need the rest.

SHARRATT: Excuse me, Sergeant Major, what do I want this rifle for?

SGT. MAJOR: If you fail, you'll go back to your company at the front.

PIERCING SOUND OF TRAIN WHISTLE. LIGHTS CONCENTRATE ON SHARRATT AT CENTRE. TRAIN SOUND ENDS – LIGHTS UP – DRUM BEAT STARTS QUIETLY.

## GREAT WAR SEQUENCE: SCENE SEVEN

AT ONE SIDE OF THE STAGE SITS AN OFFICER ON
THE BOX ATTENDED BY A CORPORAL. OFFICER IS
INTERVIEWING A SOLDIER. ENTER SHARRATT. HE
MEETS THOMAS, WHO IS WAITING FOR HIS TURN.

THOMAS: What railway company are you from?

SHARRATT: North Staffs.

THOMAS: Oh, you mean the 'arse first' railway? You
know why we call it that?

SHARRATT: No, I haven't heard that expression before.

THE SOLDIER'S INTERVIEW IS OVER. HE SALUTES
THE OFFICER AND MOVES AWAY.

THOMAS: 'Cos on your little railway you've got no
turntables, so when you travel forwards one way,
you have to travel backwards the next...arse first...

THE CORPORAL CROSSES TO THEM.

CORPORAL: Sapper Thomas!

THOMAS: Corporal!

THOMAS CROSSES STAGE TO OFFICER.

CAPTAIN: Sapper Thomas.

SHARRATT PACES UP AND DOWN.

LOUDSPEAKER VOICE ( HARRY SHARRATT): If you
fail, you'll go back to your company at the trenches.
If you fail...

THOMAS'S INTERVIEW IS OVER. HE CROSSES TO
SHARRATT IN FRONT OF CORPORAL.

THOMAS (PASSING SHARRATT): Don't forget Rule
Fifty-five.

CORPORAL : Sapper Sharratt!

SHARRATT: Corporal.

SHARRATT CROSSES TO CAPTAIN.

CAPTAIN: Sapper Sharratt!

SHARRATT (SALUTES): Sir!

DRUM BEAT STOPS.

CAPTAIN: Now, what railway do you come off?

SHARRATT: North Stafford, sir.

CAPTAIN: Oh, the 'arse first' railway, eh? Do you know why we call it that?

SHARRATT: No, sir.

CAPTAIN: Well, you see, in your small district, you go engine first one way and tender first coming back.

SHARRATT: Oh, I see, sir.

CAPTAIN: How long have you been firing?

SHARRATT: Four years, sir.

CAPTAIN: Uhhuh...and, what's in the fire box?

SHARRATT: Stays, brick arch and the fusable plugs.

CAPTAIN: Yes, anything else?

SHARRATT: No, that's the lot, sir!

CAPTAIN: Ah, now which end of the engine is the smoke box?

SHARRATT: To the front of the engine, sir.

CAPTAIN: What's in the smoke box?

SHARRATT: Blast pipe.

CAPTAIN: Yes.

SHARRATT: Tube.

CAPTAIN: Yes.

SHARRATT: Plate.

CAPTAIN: Yes.

SHARRATT: Lubrication pipes.

CAPTAIN: Yes, anything else, Sharratt?

SHARRATT: Main steam pipes, sir.

CAPTAIN: Yes, anything else, Sharratt?

SHARRATT (PAUSE): Ashes, sir?

CAPTAIN: Yes, I suppose so. Anything else, Sharratt? (PAUSE.) What happens when the driver closes the regulator?

SHARRATT: Oh yes, sir, the blower pipe.

CAPTAIN: Very good. What's Rule Fifty-five?

SHARRATT: 'When you come to a home signal at danger and you've stood there for the prescribed time and he's not pulled the signal off, the fireman will proceed to the signal box and inform the signalmen where you're standing, to see that he protects the train.' It's for the protection of the passengers, sir.

CAPTAIN: How do you know that he has protected the train?

SHARRATT: He puts a clip on the lever that protects that line.

CAPTAIN: Very good, Sapper. (PAUSE) Corporal, we'll keep this man.

LOUDSPEAKER VOICE (HARRY SHARRATT): I could have jumped over the moon.

SHARRAT CROSSES TO DRIVER BY FOOTPLATE (BARROW) TAKES OFF UNIFORM HAT AND COAT AND PUTS ON BLUE JACKET.

REST OF SOLDIERS SING ABUSE AT DRIVER AND FIREMAN

SOLDIERS (SING): We are Fred Karno's Army, no earthly good are we,
We cannot fight, we cannot shoot, no bloody good are we.
But when we get to Berlin, the Kaiser he will say
'Ah Gott, mein Gott, what a bloody fine lot are the R.O.D.R.E.!'

DRIVER (TO SOLDIERS): I was up here before you were bloody horn, see! I was up here before you thought of coming out here. (TO SHARRATT) You've got to protect yourself, see.

SCOFFING SOLDIER: Can you tell me where 'B' Company is, driver?

DRIVER: Rear four coaches...see the chef de train.

SCOFFING SOLDIER: Oooh, merci boco.

HE GOES.

DRIVER (TO SHARRATT): I'm Harry Shipley.

THEY SHAKE HANDS.

SHARRATT: Harry Sharratt.

DRIVER: What railway company were you in then?

SHARRATT: North Staffs.

DRIVER: Oh, you mean –

BOTH: – the 'arse first' railway.

DRIVER: Do you know why we call it that?

SHARRATT: Yes...I do.

LOUDSPEAKER VOICE (HARRY SHARRATT): The life in the R.O.D.s then was a wonderful life, compared with the trenches, there's no comparison at all. In spite of the slight dangers that you had.


## GREAT WAR SEQUENCE: SCENE NINE

SHARRATT: Hey, there's a lot of troops on this train. Any munitions?

DRIVER: Nah. We don't run combines. It's either munitions, troops or ambulance.

SHARRATT: How far do we take 'em?

DRIVER: Right up to the railheads. About three miles from the front line.

SHARRATT: That's pretty near, isn't it?

DRIVER: Pretty near. They could hit you with one of the eighteen-pounders...Do you speak French?

SHARRATT: French? No...

DRIVER: Well, their system is all different like. Like, you've got different signals. The stop signal is a red and white disc with four squares on it – a red and white disc with four squares on it. And then there's the biffer...

SHARRATT: The biffer?

DRIVER (SPELLS): B.I.F.U.R. That tells you there's a junction ahead. But you'll learn that in time. Anyway,

we'll start you off with the numbers...(SHARRATT
REPEATS EACH NUMBER IN FRENCH AFTER THE
DRIVER.)..one – un, two – deux, three – trois,
quatre, cinq, six, sept.

AN OFFICER ENTERS. HE SPEAKS TO SHARRATT.

OFFICER: Ah, vous! Err...quelle heure departez le
train?

DRIVER: Couple of minutes, sir.

OFFICER: Good God, you're British!

THEY CLIMB UP ONTO FOOTPLATE, VERY LOUD
STEAM HISS. ENTER COOK WITH PAN, FAST.

COOK (SHOUTING OVER NOISE OF TRAIN): Hot water
– got to make a cup of tea!

DRIVER: Get on that train, we're off.

LIGHTS CHANGE TO DARK. ROAR OF TRAIN
STARTING THEN AT SPEED. GILLIAN AND ANN
SING, VERY SOFTLY, PART OF RAILWAY LINES
WITH QUIET GUITAR ACCOMPANIMENT DURING
VOICE.

LOUDSPEAKER VOICE OVER SOUND OF TRAIN:
Some were all right, they'd be all right at the base
but that apprehension began to come one, especially
if you were going when it was getting dusk and they'd
see the flashes of the guns...

LIGHT HAS JUST FADED UP ENOUGH TO SEE
DRIVER AND FIREMAN STANDING ON FOOTPLATE
– QUIET STEAM HISS – DISTANT BARRAGE – THE
LIGHT FLICKERS ON THE FACES OF SOLDIERS
WHO HAVE COME FORWARD BY THEM.

Those flashes, they'd be twenty miles away, probably
more, you know what you can see...these flashes.
Their heads would be looking out, I felt sorry for
them.

YOUNG SOLDIER: What are those lights in the sky
across there, mate?

DRIVER: Reflections from the guns.

YOUNG SOLDIER: Well, how far are we off the trenches,
then?

DRIVER: Oh, twenty miles yet.

BLACKOUT AND HUGE BARRAGE. LIGHTS UP
THICK AND SMOKY – SOLDIERS DASH ABOUT
WITH THE STRETCHERS, KEEPING LOW – ORDERLY
CHECKS A LIST WITH A MEDICAL OFFICER.

MEDICAL ORDERLY (READING OUT): 418, Adams,
shrapnel wounds in left shoulder. 712, Bradshaw,
extensive head and face wounds. 621, Campbell,
shellshock. 109, Davidson, smashed right knee. 321,
Harrison, loss of sight, right eye. 517, Hopkins,
Sgt., fractured ribs and collar bone. 494, Jones,
loss of right leg and severe mutilation of left. 226,
McDonald, shellshock. 992, Smith, James, shrapnel
wounds and severe burns...

DRIVER (TO FIREMAN BOTH WAITING ON FOOTPLATE):
We'll have to go careful now. They'll be operating on
the train. Emergency cases from the battle. You'll
see the notices about. We've got to stop so we wouldn't
spill a glass of wine.

MEDICAL ORDERLY: ...375, Smith, John, smashed foot.
414, Watson, blinded by shrapnel, both eyes. 826,
Young, Sgt., shellshock. That's the lot for today.

CORPORAL: Carry on to Amiens to start with. Instructions there.

DRIVER: Right.

LIGHTS CHANGE – WARMER GLOW OF PLATFORM
AT NIGHT – SOME OF SOLDIERS NOW APPEAR
BACK IN RAILWAY UNIFORM.


GREAT WAR SEQUENCE: SCENE TEN

TWO RAILWAYMEN WAIT FOR A TRAIN.

LOUDSPEAKER VOICE (HERBERT SWETNAM): I remember the first time, which hasn't been mentioned
before, the ambulance train arrived at Stoke Station
to discharge the wounded soldiers from the front.

RAILWAYMAN CROSSES STAGE.

Some of them came in the night and some of them came
different parts of the day.

SOUND OF TRAIN – APPROACHES AND STOPS –
GENTLE STEAM HISS THROUGHOUT SCENE FROM
NOW ON. SOME CARRIAGE DOORS BANG AND
QUIET CONVERSATION SOUNDS. TWO RAILWAY-
MEN BRING STRETCHER ACROSS.

The first train was just the vans and they were on
the floors and on the stretchers sitting down and some
were in a bad way. Some of them were very bad, oh
yes, some of them were. They were a mixed bag.

No one was allowed on the platform, only first aid
men to assist these wounded soldiers and we used
to pick-a-back them or carry them on stretchers to
the North end, er, the South end of Stoke Station,
where the Post Office used to be.

RAILWAYMEN PUT STRETCHER DOWN AND AR-
RANGE BLANKET ROUND SOLDIER ON IT.

A LADY ENTERS.

They were right from the front, right from the front.
They was, er, got mud on them a lot of them and
First Aid treatment you know, not medically treated,
First Aid treated. Right from the front.

THE LADY CROSSES TO SOLDIER AND STRETCHER.
A LAD ENTERS AND ANOTHER WOUNDED SOLDIER
WITH ONE ARM.

LOUDSPEAKER VOICE (VIC CRITCHLOW): Well, there
were various cases, you would see some men with
their legs strapped up and stretched up. See others
with their arm in a sling...some you would notice
minus a limb of one sort or another.

THE LAD GOES TO SOLDIER ON STRETCHER.
LOOKS AT HIM.

LOUDSPEAKER VOICE (BADEN POWELL): And as a
boy I was very much interested in seeing these and
on several occasions I've gone round, there was a
lady but I couldn't say now who she was.

LADY (GIVING LAD A TIN OF CIGARETTES): I would
like you to go round and offer the soldiers a cigarette. Those who are allowed to smoke.

LAD GIVES SECOND SOLDIER A CIGARETTE. HE
LIGHTS IT.

LOUDSPEAKER VOICE (BADEN POWELL): And I think that was a very happy time for me, 'cos I saw the soldiers as could take some small comfort of pleasure.

THE LAD AND THE LADY GO OFF.

LOUDSPEAKER VOICE (VIC CRITCHLOW): But there were occasions when people hadn't a clue as to where they were.

THIRD WOUNDED SOLDIER WANDERS ACROSS, LOOKS LOST. RAILWAYMAN APPROACHES HIM WITH PAD AND PENCIL. THEY SIT TOGETHER ON BARROW AND RAILWAYMAN WRITES FOR HIM.

...asking where they were, what part of the country they were in, how they could get letters away and so on. There were occasions when people were not too badly injured, they could have letters written, asking if we would post them for them. Poor fellers, they hadn't even a stamp on them. Stamped them and posted them for them and got them away, hoped for the best that the news got through.

RAILWAYMAN SEES OFF THE LOST SOLDIER. THE LAD CROSSES TO THE SECOND WOUNDED SOLDIER. HE POINTS OFFSTAGE. HARSH GUITAR SOUND FROM SCENE NINE BEGINS VERY QUIETLY. THE VOICE SPEAKS VERY SLOWLY AND WITH A LOT OF HESITATION.

LOUDSPEAKER VOICE (BADEN POWELL): Oh, they were in very bad states in some cases but there was, on one occasion, two that were never left alone and I made enquiries what they were doing and how things had worked out for them and they told me as it was shell shock. But they looked terrible to me, they were all shaking and their heads were nodding and, if that is war, I hope as it never comes to me in that way.

SILENCE. THEN TWO GUITARS BEGIN INSTRUMENTAL ACCOMPANIMENT TO VICTORY BALL. ONE ARMED SOLDIER REMOVES HIS MILITARY JACKET AND MOVES TO CENTRE AS THE REST OF THE MEN CLEAR AWAY THE MILITARY GEAR. THE VICTORY BALL IS SPOKEN, TO THE AUDIENCE, OVER THE ACCOM-PANIMENT WHICH IS IN WALTZ TIME.

## THE VICTORY BALL

SOLDIER: The fighting was finished
    And peace was declared,
    The crowd idly gathered,
    As crowds do, and stared
    At a building illumined
    With a great brilliant light,
    Whence the music proclaimed
    Of a gay festive night.
    By motor or carriage
    The dancers arrive,
    Their adornments denoting
    Even on war some will thrive.
    The crowd stands amazed
    At the sight of it all;
    Midst their suffering and loss
    'Tis a Victory Ball.

    ACCOMPANIMENT QUIETER, FREE TIME

    To this sad-faced young widow,
    With babe at her breast,
    The scene must recall
    Thoughts of him she loved best;
    And his last parting words
    Ring again in her ear:
    'If I fall in the fight,
    They'll be kind to you, dear'.
    Thus their kindness is shown
    To that poor aching soul,
    Theirs is riches to flaunt,
    Hers a pitiful dole.
    They in jewels arrayed,
    She an old tattered shawl –
    Christ have mercy on those
    At that Victory Ball.

    WALTZ STRONGER AGAIN NOW.

    A demobilized Tommy
    Stood by in the crowd,
    And when asked his opinion
    He spoke it out loud:
    'Why, Guv'nor, this here's
    Just an insult and crime
    'Gainst the lads buried there
    'Midst the mud and the slime.

Work they refuse us,'
He bitterly said,
'Yet for them and their kind
We have fought, aye, and bled.
They may want us again,
Let them want, that is all,
To 'ell with the lot
And their Victory Ball'.

HE GOES OFF. BUSY PLATFORM NOISES.


## 1919 STRIKE

MINER, FOOTBALL MANGER, MILL GIRL, ACTRESS,
COME ON. A PORTER ENTERS WITH BARROW, WITH
ACTRESS'S CASE.

LOUDSPEAKER VOICE: This is Stoke-on-Trent. Station
Announcer calling. The train now standing at Platform
One is the eight-ten Express from Manchester to Lon-
don, Euston, calling at Stafford, Lichfield, Tamworth,
Nuneaton and Rugby, then London. This train conveys
a restaurant car.

FOOTBALL MANAGER AND ACTRESS GO OFF.

PORTER: The train now standing in Number Three Bay
is the Loop Line train to Kidsgrove, calling at: -
Etruria, Hanley, Waterloo Road, Cobridge, Burslem,
Tunstall, Pitts Hill, Newchapel and Goldenhill,
Kidsgrove Halt, Kidsgrove.

THE REST OF THE PASSENGERS GO OFF. THE
PORTER IS ABOUT TO FOLLOW WITH THE BARROW.

LOUDSPEAKER ANNOUNCEMENT: News Flash! Saturday the twenty-seventh of September nineteen-nineteen.
Railway Strike. (PORTER PUTS DOWN BARROW,
PASSENGERS RE-ENTER.) Train services suspended.
National stoppage. Like other railways throughout
the country, the North Staffordshire system is para-
lysed. In contrast to the busy scenes always in ev-
idence, Stoke Station presented a most dismal appearance, when a Sentinel representative visited it
this moring.

A REPORTER ENTERS WITH NOTEBOOK. THE
UNION SECRETARY ENTERS.

MINER (TO PORTER): Hey, what am I supposed to do, mate? How am I going to get to the Mossfield Colliery? It's all right you sitting on your arse all day. What about the rest of the working men?

FOOTBALL MANAGER: I, the Manager of Port Vale, would like you to understand that this railway business will cause a serious loss to your club, both in time and money. Do you know that we will have to travel by taxi to play United at Old Trafford!

MILL GIRL: Please, I can't get to me mill at Leek and I haven't got the bus fare.

ACTRESS (CALLING THE REPORTER TO HERE): Come here, young man! I would like it to be known to your paper that I am seriously displeased at this farcial railway situation. I, Mrs Pitt Hardacre, of the Chinese Puzzle Company, lately at the Theatre Royal, will have to travel from Hanley to Swansea in a motor lorry. What is the Government doing about it?

THE PORTER SHRUGS, LOOKS AT THE UNION SECRETARY.

FOOTBALL MANAGER: It's all right for you to shrug your shoulders and look smug but it's your sort that have brought soldiers to the Potteries. I thought we had had enough of uniforms, their presence is absolutely unnecessary and will create industrial unrest and a bad impression. They should be removed to their proper quarters. You are the cause of all this.

MILL GIRL: And another thing, you know we'll lose the Loop Line, and that will be a tragedy. It was a grand little system, a service every twenty minutes and the nicest little stations in the country. You can't, you just can't.

ENTER W.D.PHILLIPS.

REPORTER: Mr Phillips I believe this is the week of your retirement, after many years at the helm of the North Staffordshire Railway Railway Company.

W.D: Yes, thirty-seven years.

REPORTER: What are your feelings, Mr Phillips, about this railway strike?

W.D: I feel sad to be retiring from active service with

the old North Stafford, under the present circumstances. I am not an enemy of the Trade Unions. I have said to their representatives 'Go away and come back to me when you represent the majority of the railwaymen.' and they've come back. But I can recall no strike entered into so lightly with so little justification and with such entire disregard for the public interest. The Government begged the Railway Union to postpone their strike were it only for two or three days.

REPORTER: What was the Union's reply, Mr Phillips?

W.D. (TO UNION SECRETARY): They declined to grant even this respite to their fellow countryment and a service, upon which the life of a whole people so much depends, was stopped without practically any warning.

UNION SECRETARY: Let me remind the Nation of two facts, as to which there can be no controversy. Firstly, the railway workers are suffering from the strike, as much as other people are. If the general Public starves, they starve with it. It is therefore silly to pretend that the railway workers aim at starving out a garrison, of which they themselves form a part. Secondly, it is mischievous as well as absurd to pretend that our railway system is a Public Service. It is a private speculation and has always been conducted by its proprietors, with as little regard to the welfare of the nation, as to the conditions of the employees. Look, we've had enough of private speculation. The war was a private speculation. What had we got to do with it, except to go out and be mowed down? To attempt to persuade the public that, in resisting a private interest so unscrupulous, we are attacking the life of the nation and rebelling against the state, deserting our duty as public servants and engaging in an anarchist conspiracy, is to treat the nation as both ignorant and gullible. The dispute over this very modest demand has ended in a nation having very unwillingly to try the experiment of doing without us for a while and eventually doing without the private companies. We think the nation will find us the greater loss.

ALL GO EXCEPT THE UNION SECRETARY AND THE PORTER. TWO GUITARS BEGIN ACCOMPANIMENT TO AMALGAMATION SCENE, JEFF AND THE FOUR GIRLS STAND UP AND LOOK AT THE LOUDSPEAKER.

AMALGAMATION SCENE

LOUDSPEAKER ANNOUNCEMENT: Railway Act, nineteen
twenty-one. With a view to the re-organisation and
more efficient and economical working of the railways
of Great Britain, railways shall be formed into groups
in accordance with the provision of this Act and the
principal railway companies in each group shall be
amalgamated, the North Staffordshire Railway Company to form a part of the London, Midland and
Scottish Railway.

FOUR RAILWAYMEN (FORMERLY DRIVER, SHUNTER,
LAD, UNION SECRETARY) FORM A SEMICIRCLE
OPPOSITE JEFF AND GIRLS.

JEFF AND ALL FOUR GIRLS WITH TWO GUITARS
ACCOMPANYING: In the year of nineteen twenty-
three,
Amalgamation came to be,
Strangers came into the sheds,
Different caps to different heads.

Goodbye to days of Knotty fame,
Engine bearing driver's name,
The loss for some was hard to take,
Golden sovereigns hard to make.

ALL FOUR GIRLS (CHANT WITH GUITAR): North Stafford-
shire Railway Loopi-la
I call Platform Three.
North Staffordshire Railway Loopi-la
I call Platform Four.

GUITAR STOPS. AS EACH MAN SPEAKS HE TAKES
OFF HIS JACKET, FOLDS IT UP AND PUTS HIS
HAT ON TOP OF IT ON THE FLOOR IN FRONT OF
HIM.

DRIVER: We'd lost our identity to start with. There was
an influx of new people, a new set of men all together.
The old railway, as we knew it, had gone for good.

FOUR GIRLS (CHANT WITH GUITAR): North Staffordshire Railway Loopi-la
I call Platform Five.

GUITAR STOPS.

DRIVER: Things went pretty normal, aye, normal for

about twelve months after the amalgamation, till they got it all weighed up. Then they started. Looking after the profits. They shut up all the shops.

FIREMAN: Actually speaking, when the amalgamation come off y'see, Stoke automatically lost a lot of jobs. A job that Stoke men used to use, well Crewe men collared them, Derby men collared them, Stafford men collared them, Macclesfield men collared them, you see. All these outside districts, like the Midland and North Western, come in and collared the jobs and automatically you lost a lot of work with that, you see. Crewe men, see, and Derby men used to come in, see, and take the jobs. I mean, it wasn't an advantage to us at all. It was like, instead of promotion, it was like you was put back a bit. That's how things went. Course, when you amalgamate with anything, like that, somebody is going to lose a good job and that's how things run, with amalgamation.

FOUR GIRLS (WITH GUITAR): North Staffordshire Railway Loopi-la,
I call Platform Six.

GUITAR STOPS.

LAD: When we worked on The Knotty there was a voluntary organisation, the St John's Ambulance. They encouraged you, if you were interested. The Newcastle St John's Section was very enthusiastic. They turned up every Sunday morning for practice...We were very enthusiastic. The Newcastle team won the North Staffordshire Railway Directors' Shield for seven years running, then Blythe Bridge for two years, then Newcastle won it back for two years off them. After the Knotty they didn't allow us to be Brigade men, they didn't support us.

ENTER F.A.L.BARNWELL AND W.D.PHILLIPS.

FOUR GIRLS (WITH GUITAR): North Staffordshire Railway Loopi-la,
I call Platform Seven.

GUITAR CONTINUES UNDER BARNWELL'S SPEECH.

BARNWELL: F.A.L.Barnwell, General Manager, In my capacity as Mr Phillip's Deputy, I have know many of you for a long time and I want to talk to two classes.

First, there are the men of the future, who are going
into the services of the London, Midland and Scottish
Railways and who will have to carry on the traditions
of the old North Staffordshire Company. You might
find things rather different in the future but I hope you
will remember the spirit of the North Stafford and
carry it with you into the London, Midland and Scottish
Railway.

The other class to whom I refer are those who are
resting in the evening of their days, after work well
done, and I envy them. There are those too, who are
waiting on the border line, worrying a little. But they
need not hide their faces as the old line passes out.
For she throughout kept true to her great traditions
and carried her colours to the end.

HE SHAKES HANDS WITH EACH OF THE FOUR
RAILWAYMEN.

FOUR GIRLS (CHANT WITH GUITAR): North Stafford-
shire Railway Loopi-la,
I call Platform Eight.
North Staffordshire Railway Loopi-la,
I call Platform Nine.

GUITAR ENDS. BARNWELL AND W.D. SALUTE THE
MEN WITH A FINAL WAVE, ALL EXCEPT UNION
SECRETARY RAILWAYMAN MOVE TO SIDE OF STAGE.

UNION SECRETARY: They used to send these big engines
round the Loop, the L.M.S. did. Well, they weren't
built for the job and the Loop Line wouldn't take them.
They had no end of derailments with these big engines.
They used to come off, the curves were too sharp for
them, see. Well, these little locos that the Knotty
built were built specially for the track, see. There's
a lot of sharp curves on the Loop Line, you know.
And they used to send these big engines with a big
wheel base, wouldn't go round the curves.

Amalgamation was the biggest mistake as ever was made.
I'll tell you that. When they used to send these outside locos on the job and they come off, we used to
say 'Send for a bloody Knotty. That'd shift it.'
And it did.

GUITAR STARTS AGAIN.

FOUR GIRLS: North Staffordshire Railway Loopi-la,
  I call Platform Ten.

  ALL CAST FORM UP IN TWO OPPOSING LINES.

JEFF AND FOUR GIRLS (SING): Goodbye to days of Knotty
  fame,
  Engine bearing driver's name,
  The loss for some was hard to take,
  Golden sovereigns hard to make.

ALL SING: Farewell to the world of W.D.
  Of tip your hat for courtesy,
  The personal touch on the personal line
  The N.S.R. was lost to time.

JEFF AND FOUR GIRLS (SING): In the year of nineteen
  twenty-three
  Amalgamation came to be
  Strangers came into the sheds,
  Different caps to different heads.

ALL SING: Farewell to the world of W.D.
  Of tip your hat for courtesy,
  The personal touch on the personal line
  The N.S.R. was lost to time.


                        THE END

NOTES ON THE SCRIPT

PART ONE

INTRODUCTION
The station announcements used the recorded voice of Vic
Critchlow, who started as a boy on the Knotty and eventually became station announcer (pre loudspeakers) at
Stoke Station. The introductory announcement is one contemporary with the first production of the show, just before electrification of the Euston–Stoke line.

INTRODUCTION SONG
Words by Jeff Parton, tune traditional Irish (Morrisey
and the Russian Sailor).

COACH SCENE
Song – THREE MERRY MEN OF KENT – words and music
anonymous, from an eighteenth century broadside.

The dialogue in the scene consists entirely of extracts
from advertisements and letters in the Staffordshire
Advertiser for the period 1800–1820, (with exclamations
added.)

DANDIES SCENE
The lady's and dandies' speeches are extracts from the
comments of Thomas Creevey M.P. after a footplate ride
on the Manchester to Liverpool line in 1929, and from
the utterances of the liveliest and most facetious op-
ponent of railways, the renowned Col. Sibthorpe M.P.
who foresaw the doom of England coming with the track.
The mandoline phrase consisted of the last line of the
song 'When the King Enjoys his Own Again' which we
had used the previous year in THE STAFFORDSHIRE
REBELS. It seemed to fit.

POTTERIES RAILWAY COMMITTEE
In Stoke-on-Trent's Reference Library in Hanley is a
small volume of neatly handwritten minutes of the
meetings of the Potteries Railway Committee. The
Committee met mostly in a large room at the Swan Inn
in the same town. It consisted of men whose names are
now world-famous as leading pottery manufacturers –
Ridgway, Wedgwood, Mason, Wood and others – and was
chaired by the Newcastle-under-Lyme M.P. and coal
pit owner, Richard Edensor Heathcote. This scene

consists of a slightly edited version of their first important resolution, shared between three characters representing the young manufacturers.

Hitting the right tone and level in the acting of this small scene proved one of the keys to a good basic tone for the whole show. It had to be conversational, candid, with no straining after irrelevant characterisation coming between the actors and the audience. It had to be concentrated and absorbed with no tense silence preventing everyone in the theatre from relaxing and listening.

## LEN PRESTON'S GRANDAD

Len Preston was the subject of one of the first interviews recorded by Peter Terson at the beginning of the research period. He started as a boy on the Knotty before the first World War and eventually worked for the LMS after Amalgamation in 1923. Like many Knotty veterans he came from a railway family – in fact in the days when railway jobs were hard to come by, it was almost the only way in. Len now lives in retirement in Newcastle–under–Lyme, and contributed a great deal to the show. He is a vigorous man in his seventies, who still does judo and once nearly wore out the actors by taking their limbering session before rehearsal.

The scene consisted of a silent demonstration of the story told by Len's voice over the loudspeakver, interrupted by the live dialogue between Grandad and Engineer. The scene was created from a section of the tape recording of the original interview but had to be re-recorded to improve the audibility of the recording with a little loss of spontaneity. This is one of the hazards of this kind of work, as the careful circumstances which get the best results from a quality point of view often inhibit the person being interviewed.

## STEPHENSON SCENE

The words and music of the song were composed by Peter Terson, himself a Geordie. The Stephenson speeches are by George Stephenson and were gathered from a number of biographies of him.

## STEPHENSON'S REPORT

It is a tribute to the succinctness of Stephenson's English that his actual report, only very slightly edited in two or three places, provides the dialogue for a scene that was watched in a concentrated silence which surprised us in Stoke at first, but amazed us in Florence, where the place names meant nothing at all. No concession was ever made in the direction of making the scene comprehensible to people from outside the district. There was no point. In Italy we took the risk (as with the whole show) and it worked.

TOWNS UPON A HILL
Words of the song are by Peter Terson, to a tune by Anne Raitt and Gillian Brown. The song was partly inspired by a locally famous autobiography of a man who worked as a child in the potworks in the 1840's called WHEN I WAS A CHILD. This book by 'An Old Potter' also provided Arnold Bennett with two chapters in the first book of his novel CLAYHANGER (4 and5).

OAK FARM SCENE
This scene was much modified during the three year life of THE KNOTTY. The aim was to present the story of the purchase of the site of Crewe station by the Nantwich lawyer, but the scene began life in 1966 as a kind of cabaret turn by the first actor to play narrator – Peter King. He is a talented mime and improviser and turned it into a kind of solo spot with topical allusions. By the first revival of the show in 1967 Peter had left the company and the new farmer, Robert French, contributed an amazing doggerel melodrama which worked as well as the old version and tended to stick to the point of the scene. It is the only 'written' scene in the show. The story of the purchase came from the Stafford-shire Advertiser of 15 November 1845.

SURVEYORS POLE DANCE AND SONG
The words of the song were adapted from a verse by a North Staffordshire poet about some railway speculators from Leek. The tune is traditional Irish ('Banks of the Roses'). The dance was inspired by the jogging rhythm of the song and was an attempt to demonstrate the complex situation which left the smaller North Staffordshire Railway Company intact after a period of frantic speculation and take-over bids by three of the large companies. The scene was always a particular success and won a great round of applause, sometimes even that theatrical delight, a final roar of laughter which creams off into loud clapping. Like all such jobs involving carefully timed movements to music, it took about ten times the rehearsal time of the average dramatic scene. But it was worth it.

WOLSELEY V. WOOD
In this scene we created a physical and private confron-
tation from one which so far as we know only took place
in the pages of the Staffordshire Advertiser and in the
political arena. The two men may never even have met.
They certainly took issue with one another, and their
argument seemed to encapsulize the historical confron-
tation of the opposing interests of landowner and manufacturer that was brought about by the coming of the railway.

Sir Charles wrote a hot letter to the Staffordshire
Advertiser which was printed on 28 April 1838. Shortly
afterwards Enoch Wood replied to it at a public meeting
of the Potteries Railway Committee. The two first actors
Wolseley and Wood, Ellis Dale and Ron Daniels, created
the scene by editing together extracts from these two
sources with other relevant material from the same newspaper. The tea business was put in to give some forma-
lity and therefore tension as well as naturalistic detail
to the scene after a number of stylized and relaxed epi-
sodes.

PADDY WORKS ON THE RAILWAY
This is probably the most famous British folk song
about the building of the railways. It was only slightly
amended by the insertion of 'Stoke' in the last verse.

CUTTING THE FIRST SOD
This scene was based on the account of the confused
proceedings in the Staffordshire Advertiser of 26 September 1846. Its basic style represents one straight-
forward way of representing a complex and crowded
incident on stage – simple demonstrative mime to a
narration. Its success depends obviously on how well
it is done and again, like the Pole Dance, rehearsal
consumed a fair amount of time. Its mocking attitude
can be a dangerous one – it is only too easy in the
documentary to try to make such incidents funny,
taking the nervous way out, afraid of commitment, of
putting oneself in the vulnerable position of just being
serious. But I think though some other scenes were
based on an ironic attitude to the event this is the only
one which actually abused the incident by describing
it as a farce. The attitude in fact grew naturally from
the pompous tones of the newspaper in contrast to the
obviously disorderly chaos of the ceremony, all con-

fusion and bent spades and fine speeches in a sea of mud. It seems an obvious thing to say but in discovering the way to stage a scene we always tried to make a sensitive response to the nature of the incident represented and the quality of the source material describing it.

NAVVY SONG
Jeff Parton wrote the words of this song to the tune of the ancient Earlsdon Sword Dance.

NAVVY SEQUENCE
This sequence was presented so that the audience saw and heard first the attitudes of the articulate North Staffordshire public whose contact with the navvies was fearfully remote (and often through the Court case section of the newspaper). The women's and gentlemen's speeches are an edited collection from local Court cases and other contemporay descriptions. Terry Coleman's book THE RAILWAY NAVVIES, now published as a Penguin, was a useful guide to primary source material here.

Then we tried to show a gang of navvies who may have worked on the Harecastle tunnel answering for themselves. The sources here are varied. The first Navvy's speech is the only playwright-written speech in the show, being provided by Peter Terson to fill a gap. The second Navvy's speech is a version by the first actor to play it, Edward Clayton, of a description of Harecastle tunnel and an accident from the Staffordshire Advertiser. The scene between the young navvy and his wife was worked out by Peter King and Susan Pitts from advertisements in the temperance magazine provided for the navvies by a group of religious people. The temperance poem comes from the same paper and the vicar's questions are asked in it by the Rev. D.W. Barrett, a navvies' chaplain. Jeremiah Cumm's case is from the Staffordshire Advertiser.

This sequence leaned heavily (and somewhat dully I always felt) on recorded announcements which used progress reports from the Advertiser.

QUEUE SCENE
This scene was created by two of the first girls in the cast (Angula Harman and Susan Pitts) by editing together pieces of research material collected by Peter

Terson from the Advertiser for the period of the Railway Opening and linking them with a little probable queue dialogue which was as much the result of improvisation as anything else. Improvisation in this accepted theatrical sense of the word is a technique we use only rarely in creating the documentaries.

## HURRAH FOR STEAM
(Words of song by Dick Barton, tune by Jeff Parton.) This song began life as a kind of hearty number with a chorus of 'Whistle and Shout...' but our enthusiasm for this version diminished and for the third (1969) revival we decided to try a four part setting to be sung like a formal quartet, making the coming of steam sound a bit more stately for a change, as well as providing the right mood for the posh banquet.

## BANQUET SCENE
The enthusiastic speeches came from the newspaper reports of the banquet to celebrate the opening of the Crewe and Congleton branches on 9 October 1848, plus some extracts from an earlier speech of Enoch Wood's at a meeting of the Potteries Railway Committee. Copeland's speech is derived from an account of the advantages of the railways to the manufacturers, lightly elaborated for a laugh. The lyrical concluding speech is from the Advertiser.

## RAILWAY LINES
This song was written by Gillian Brown almost to order. At the start of rehearsals we had made a running list of songs and scenes knowing what job we wanted each one to do. We had decided that the first part was to end with a song which said 'We've built these lines, where will they lead?' I felt we needed something dry, astringent. I also felt we could do with Brecht and Weill.

Gillian Brown and Anne Raitt, from Colchester and Edinburgh respectivelly, had joined the company together earlier that year after spending a year unemployed, occasionally managing to get singing engagements in folk clubs. THE KNOTTY was ultimately almost pivotted round their painstaking musicianship, and I never cease to wonder at how well these two fine actresses sing together.

Gillian and Anne went away and slaved at the job of making me not regret the absence of Lotte Lenya. Sev-

eral days later they announced that the new song was
ready, and stepped into the middle of the acting area to
run through it in a break in the rehearsal. It was unaccompanied, the two girls singing almost flawlessly
together sometimes in unison, sometimes in an almost
discordant interval, a process in which the music was
used to penetrate and illuminate the words in the manner
of the best of folk song. The theatre was brought to
a reverent standstill. Their performance of the song
remained one of the unforgettable moments of the show.


PART TWO

NORTH STAFFORDSHIRE RAILWAY LOOPI LA
The Loop Line, which provided the equivalent of a twenty
minute bus service for the northern and central towns of
the Potteries was opened in 1873. It took the form of a
crescent leaving the main Crewe line just north of Stoke
Station and rejoining it beyond Goldenhill. The track has
only just stopped being used (in 1970) and has been
bought by the City of Stoke-on-Trent to make a walk way
linking several of the City's Parks in an imaginative
reclamation scheme. The recorded chant used to open
the Second Part was the most popular of a number of
skipping songs about the Knotty still to be heard in 1966
when we recorded the one we used in the playground of
Berryhill County Junior School. It provided the original
inspiration in fact for this documentary. The chant has
now (in 1970) been ousted by an accidentally defiant one
which begins 'North Staffordshire British Railways...'

INTRODUCTION SONG
Words by Jeff Parton, tune traditional Irish ('Morrisey
and the Russian Sailor')

W.D.PHILLIPS INTERVIEW
(from the Railway Magazine, February 1899, with small
additions by Peter King and Ellis Dale.)

Though research was done evenly over the whole period
of the line's independent existence to 1923, just before
rehearsals began we decided to skip a detailed narrative
of the period between the opening of the first section of
the track and a portrait of the railway at the beginning of
the new century. This was the period dominated by its
legendary General Manager W. D. Phillips, and remembered vividly by the many retired railwaymen we

interviewed who began their working lives during that
period as boys. W.D.Phillips had been a pupil of the
Scott Russell shipyards at Millwall, where he worked
on the Great Eastern steamship with Isambard Brunel.
When he took up his post with the North Stafford he was
the youngest Railway Manager in the country. His talents
undoubtedly helped to keep the small company surviving
independently for so long. He constantly walked the
track from end to end popping up when least expected
and adding another caustic remark to a memorable
collection. One signalman would warn the next of his
approach by a special signal not in the rule book – ONE
PAUSE TWO. 'Bob me on, Signalman' W.D. sometimes
cracked as he left a box. Some kind of infirmity re-
sulted in his tilting his head a little to one side, a
feature always carefully reproduced by his now ven-
erable imitators. He seems to have been tough but fair,
and much respected for his straightness, his insistence
on providing equal promotion opportunities for railwaymen with only elementary education, and the fact that
he never forgot a face and always greeted it, apparently
insisting on the same practice in others 'A railwayman
will always observe the courtesies to another railwayman...' (COURTESY TALE)

FIRST DAY ON THE LINE
Fred Adams told us how he had left working on the
potbanks as soon as he got the chance of a job on the
railway. This was a matter of being recommended by
a father or an uncle, or being able to provide about
three testimonials. Even then you were lucky to get on.
Nowadays a girl who gets a job as an air hostess has
her picture in the local paper. We got the distinct
impression that the railway stations of those days were
more like our swinging airports than the battered platforms which give us a picture of that bygone age today.
Christopher Martin wrote this song, basing it on our
interview with Fred, and Anne Raitt and Gillian Brown
made the tune.

PEELINGS TALE
This story about Ross Holland, another Knotty character, is a transcript from Peter Terson's first tape
recorded interview with Len Preston. Again it seems
an obvious thing to say but verbatim transcripts of
tape recordings make amazingly vigorous and speakable

theatre dialogue. Handling this kind of material demonstrates the striking differences between the oral and the
written English language. (The Amalgamation Scene
provides another example which made richly effective
theatre.)

BELL TEST
A section of a page from the North Staffordshire Railway Company's rule book detailing signalman's bell
signals in question (words) answer (bells) form provided
the dialogue for this scene, with the addition of the last
hesitation and answering quip.

KNOCKING UP
Harry Sharratt, a retired driver who was on the theatre
staff, provided us with much interesting material and we
used his recorded voice in this scene, at the start of a
kind of night shift section which lasted to the end of the
shunting sequence.

MOON SONG
(Words and music by Sir Jules Benedict)

This was a favourite Edwardian ballad which Frank
Oakes (traffic) and Harry Sharratt (driver) told us they
used to sing together in the shunting yards and on the
footplate on the night shift, along with WATCHMAN WHAT
OF THE NIGHT? The business of sorting mailbags in
the scene began as another item of railway description
but developed into an effective poker-faced comic ritual
in the hands of the first two actors Edward Clayton and
Ellis Dale. Neither acknowledged each other's presence
except by singing together, nor smiled at all, from beginning to end.

UNION MEETINGS AND SHUNTING SEQUENCE
A theatrical description of shunting in a goods yard at
night provided the means of linking material that would
make a narrative of the rise of the railway trade unions
at the beginning of the century. Dialogue for these
sequences, leading to the 1911 railway strike, and for
the later 1919 strike, were collated from three sources
by Ron Daniels, who played the Driver in the original
production. We had been lent the manuscript minutes of
the first Stoke meetings of ASLEF, the footplate union.
We also had a great deal of material in our tape recorded
interviews on the subject, particularly from Tom Underwood, another athletic seventy-year-old and militant

though unorthodox Socialist. The local <u>Evening Sentinel</u> now existed, in those days a vigorous and radical newspaper, and provided public statements, news from other areas, and descriptions of the strike. Vic Critchlow another retired North Stafford man rehearsed the shunter in the bewildering use of pole, swivelling lamp and the pealess whistle which produced the coded signals to the signalman to switch points to the different sections.

There is probably more invented dialogue in these sections – improvised or written by Ron Daniels and the first actors of the scenes – than in others though in terms of the number of words involved it adds up to about an eighth of the total. Our sources for Part Two were less formal, and a more naturalistic style developed which seemed appropriate to the difference in mood of the historical period. At the most a phrase or a sentence might link two phrases or sentences from a tape recording transcript or a newspaper extract, and some grammatical modification take place in say the tense of the verbs involved, to link the two. It is at this point that the work gets nearest to writing and where the difference between the EDITING processes which characterize these documentaries and the WRITING of a play is nearly one of degree only and not of kind. But it remains a distinct and important difference.

CHAIRMAN'S SPEECH
Taken from the report in the <u>Evening Sentinel</u> 9 August 1911.

W.D's RABBIT
In this scene Christopher Martin, who played the part throughout the three-year life of the documentary simply tells the most famous W.D.Phillips story. For performances in Florence the scene was played in Italian, where the first night audience applauded every imperfectly pronounced phrase.

GOLDEN SOVEREIGNS
Fred Adams voice was used to describe the balmy days of lavish tipping. It seemed an appropriate end to the paternalistic period before the first Railway Strike and the beginnings of a modern industrial structure.

1911 RAILWAY STRIKE SONG
Words by Christoper Martin to a tune by Gillian Brown.

The 1911 Strike was fought to secure recognition of the Trade Unions by the railway companies. Tom Underwood told us that the only thing he remembered of the 1911 strike as a boy was chalking WE WANT RECOGNITION on the pavements. The appearance of W.D. seemed an inevitable (if apocryphal) addition.

PICKET SCENE
ASLEF minutes and a series of statements by both sides of the dispute printed in the Evening Sentinel provided all the speeches in the Picket scene.

LAMENT OF THE FOOTPLATE MEN
This song was created by dovetailing together two ironic poems by a railwayman poet (not a local man for once) F.W.Skerrett – ENGINE DRIVING AS IT IS and THE FIRE-MAN'S GROWL. Jeff Parton did the job, fitting the song to the tune THE BEGGARMAN.

GREAT WAR
In our conversations with North Stafford veterans the First World War was revealed as a watershed in the history of the railway as in almost every other sector of society. It was easier to get into the railway after the war, and the old men complained of a drop in the standard of the men who joined. Amalgamation in 1923 was an almost inevitable re-sult of emergency wartime grouping – a kind of temporary nationalisation to facilitate troop movements. The sourer terms on which the 1919 Strike was fought are a part of the workingman's post-war bitterness.

Another starting point of the documentary was provided by the reminiscences of the late Harry Sharratt, a retired driver on the Victoria Theatre staff. It seemed logical to follow to France one of the many railwaymen who fought on the footplate, driving troop or munitions trains up to the front line railheads and bringing back the dismal cargo of maimed soldiers. Harry worked closely with us in re-hearsals, recalling incidents he had been involved in, providing dialogue from his memories direct to the actors on the set. We used Harry's voice from time to time to provide the thoughts of the young Harry, played on stage by Christopher Martin. The device of keeping the actors in a wide circle on the stage throughout the sequence, simply coming into the centre or across it to play a scene and moving back to the edge at the end was necessitated by the fact that the narrative consisted for the most part of a series of very short incidents. These often comprised a single sentence only, a significant gesture like picking up a rifle from the armoury, or a three-line anecdote. The free-ranging narrative movement that the open circle of theatre in the round permits is made even more flexible by this kind of technique (which is of course <u>primitive</u> rather than original.) Its story telling possibilities are very exciting.

VICTORY BALL
This is another and characteristic poem by F.W.Skerrett which was spoken to a waltz tune by Jeff Parton.

1919 STRIKE
By the time of the second great national railway strike railways were no longer an innovation. The daily lives of a huge proportion of the population depended on the service. The railway workers had at last some real power in their hands. When they withdrew their labour in 1919 the public clamoured bitterly. The official statements of the Unions and the Companies were almost drowned in the outcry from immobilised passengers. Ron Daniels (who played the <u>Sentinel</u> Reporter in this scene) reenacted the process which filled the <u>Sentinel</u> in September 1919 with their complaints.

The strike occurred ironically during the very week of W.D.Phillips' retirement. His published comments were added to in this scene by some remarks on the Trade Unions he had made earlier, recalled by Harry Sharratt who had been a close friend of W.D.'s personal assistant. The final speech spoken by the Union Secretary was in fact made by the great NUR leader J.H. Thomas one of the first working man M.P.'s and ill-fated Chancellor in the first Labour Government.

AMALGAMATION SONG
Words by Christopher Martin with tune by Jeff Parton.

AMALGAMATION SCENE
On the last Saturday morning before our first night on the following Tuesday the show as usual was just being completed. As a stopgap I decided to get the actors simply to speak the transcribed speeches of the old men who had remembered their feelings 'when Amalgamation came about' and include some of the emotional speech by the new General Manager, Barnwell. It was the first time we had used our oral material at any length, seriously. They were to be plain statements by actors standing still, talking to the audience as they took off coat and cap with the Knotty badge for the last time. The great fear was that it would sound

both corny and, much worse, patronising. It didn't.
Providing the actors didn't characterize and let the
speeches speak for themselves it made one of the most
eloquent scenes in the documentary.

Amalgamation with LNWR and other companies to form
the LMS left the country with four large railway companies
– LMS, LNER, GWR, and SR. As well as the larger
political and economic consequences it was the end of
the period which has become a legend among railwaymen
in the Potteries. The little Knotty with its tankies, the
drivers who had their own engines, the guards with their
names on the brake vans, the 'old man', the family feeling,
the defiance of the surrounding giant companies. It meant
the end of the personal touch; things became numbers, the
Rifle Club was abandoned, Stoke Sheds shut down, men
dispersed, the old engines were scrapped, the crimson
of the Knotty painted black. It meant the end of the St.
John's Ambulance and the Director's Cup, the losing of
jobs, the end of the Knot.

For forty years, old Knotty men have had to see Stoke
become a lesser station, but it's with a smile that they
see it regaining its old position as the centre of things
with the coming of electrification.

'Amalgamation was the biggest mistake was ever was made.'

Ken Jackson – Permanent Way.

THE END

## ACKNOWLEDGEMENTS

Our primary source of background information for THE
KNOTTY has been the authorative work on the subject by
the joint authors of THE NORTH STAFFORDSHIRE RAIL-
WAY, 'Manifold' (the pen name of J.R.Hollick, C.A.
Moreton, G.N.Nowell-Gosling, F.M.Page, W.T.Stubbs).
We should like to thank them all, and particularly Dr.
Hollick for his unfailing co-operation and help.

The North Staffordshire Railway Association has been involved with the making of the show since the beginnings of
our research. For their reminiscences and advice we are
deeply indebted to Len Preston, Fred Adams, Tom Underwood, T.A.Stubbs, Harry Sharratt, Ken Jackson, Hughie

Ford, Chris Beech, Stan Pedley, George Collier, Ald. Gordon Dale, E. Stanely, Vic Crichlow, Herbert Swetnam, Charles Edward Dawson, Baden Powell, and also Messrs. Lawton, Stonehewer, Brown, Ball, Wilshaw, Phillips, Dykes, Mills, Power, Pope, Nind, Harding, Oakes, Jones, Powner and many other men who worked the North Staffordshire Railway.

The book THE RAILWAY NAVVIES by Terry Coleman was a great source of navvy background material and imaginative stimulus.

We are indebted to the Librarians and staff of Hanley Reference Library; the William Salt Library, Stafford; British Railways Archives, Porchester House; the House of Lords Record Office; and to the Curator of Hanley Museum and the Archivist and staff of Staffordshire County Record Office.

In our search for the skipping songs of the Knotty we were helped by the staff and pupils of Berryhill County Junior School, and Trentside C.P.School, as well as Mr P. Howell, Mrs K.Carter, Mrs Stocks; Messrs. J.F.Price, T.Wainwright, R.R.Davies, W.Hughes; the Misses Deaville, Anne Roden, Julie Whittaker, Jessie Moston, Gillian Grundy and Kathy Buckley.

We have had close and constant co-operation from Mr George Dow, formerly local Divisional Manager, British Rail and his staff, and Mr Burton, Publicity Manager at Stoke Station.

We should also like to thank Malcolm Willis, Secretary of the Railway Preservation Society (Midland Area); Mr Longdon, Display Manager of Lewis's Department Store, Hanley; Mr Holland for contribution of display railway models; Mr Robert Keyes for photographs and valuable information and guidance; Mr H.B.Oliver, of the London section of the North Staffordshire Railway Association; Ruth Noyes of the English Folk Dance and Song Society; Charles Parker, BBC Birmingham, Mrs G.Cavanagh-Mainwaring of Whitmore Hall, Mrs Tasker; Mr Tupholme, Editor of the Evening Sentinel; Wood and Sons, Burslem, the Territorial Army for advice and loan of equipment; and all those who have guided us and helped in the making of this documentary.